INTERNATIONAL AID UNDER THE MICROSCOPE

INTERNATIONAL AID UNDER THE MICROSCOPE

European Union Project Cycle Management in Jamaica

Shinique Walters

The University of the West Indies Press
Jamaica • Barbados • Trinidad and Tobago

The University of the West Indies Press
7A Gibraltar Hall Road, Mona
Kingston 7, Jamaica
www.uwipress.com

A catalogue record of this book is available from the National Library
of Jamaica.

ISBN: 978-976-640-848-0 (paper)
978-976-640-849-7 (Kindle)
978-976-640-850-3 (ePub)

Cover design by Jervis Stone

Printed in the United States of America

To my mother, Opal Davis (1960–2017)
Always a loving smile

Contents

Figures

Abbreviations

ABCD	asset-based community development
CBC	community-based contracting
CBO	community-based organization
CSJP	Community Security and Justice Programme
DFID	Department for International Development
EC	European Commission
EDF	European Development Fund
EU	European Union
GOJ	Government of Jamaica
IMF	International Monetary Fund
JSIF	Jamaica Social Investment Fund
LFA	Logical Framework Approach
MDG	Millennium Development Goal
MNSJ	Ministry of National Security and Justice
NGO	non-governmental organization
NSA	non-state actor
OECD	Organisation for Economic Cooperation and Development
PCM	Project Cycle Management
PIOJ	Planning Institute of Jamaica
PRP	Poverty Reduction Programme
SDC	Social Development Commission
UNDP	United Nation Development Programme
USAID	United States Agency for International Development

1.

Aid in Context

The provision of technical assistance, or sharing of technology or knowledge, is a major component of international development support recognized by many development pundits and some academics as an indispensable element of development. According to Seers (1969, 3), "Development occurs with the reduction and elimination of poverty, inequality and unemployment within a growing economy." International development assistance, which comes in many forms such as military intervention, project aid and foreign direct investments, facilitates several activities and requires proper management in order to be considered successful. However, different international organizations, for example, the US Agency for International Development (USAID), the World Bank, the United Nations Development Programme (UNDP) and the European Union (EU) all have their own guidelines for achieving successful project outcomes.

The European Union Project Cycle Management

The European Union is an important economic partner for least developed countries with its primary objective being the eradication of poverty as identified in the United Nations Millennium Development Goals (MDGs). The organization provides financial aid and commits to increasing this assistance guided by criteria entailed in its European Union Project Cycle Management (EU PCM) system – the main text used to govern funded social development projects.

The European Union, through its executive arm the European Commission (EC), adopted PCM in 1992 as its primary tool for project design and management, and requires the use of the Logical Framework Approach (LFA). The text, prepared in order to support ongoing improvements in the quality of EC development assistance, was further modified in 1993 and subsequently updated in 2001 and 2003 (EC 2004b). The methodology establishes the process for each of the five phases of the cycle of management, and the entire system represents guidelines for EU-funded projects and will be referenced here as EU guidelines, or simply, the guidelines.

Different components of this system are employed for initiation, implementation and evaluation of a project, and include the financial agreement, procurement guidelines, programme estimate and grant contract documents. The primary document is the financial agreement, often dubbed "the bible" since it informs the lifespan of the project from its embryonic to its evaluative stages. Based on order of usage, the procurement guidelines are next, followed by the programme estimate and finally, the grant contract.

The guidelines are expected to support the relevance, feasibility and effectiveness in the management of projects funded by the European Union. The primary objective is to promote consistency and clarity while facilitating the operational flexibility needed for a dynamic and diverse external approach in the implementation of social development projects (EC 2004b). One of the aims of the European Union in development co-operation, both for member states and at the community level, is the ability to increase aid effectiveness through coordination, harmonization and common vision.

The guidelines vary in their objectives, scope and scale based on the size and intended project impact (EC 2004b). They define and manage investments and change processes and are considered a model in their ability to design, deliver and support the implementation of interventions of the highest possible quality. The guidelines also cover the whole project cycle, which is planning, adoption, design, implementation, application (including enforcement), evaluation and revisions. All EU interventions aim to achieve certain objectives through one or several means, in line with the specifications set by the EU Treaty (EC 2004b).

These guidelines were prepared to encourage improvement in the quality of EC development assistance. In this regard, quality is defined in terms of the relevance, feasibility and effectiveness of the programmes and projects supported with EC funds, including how well they are managed (EC 2004b). To ensure quality in their intervention programmes, the European Union uses five pillars of assessment: relevance, sustainability, impact assessment, efficiency and effectiveness. Good management practices and effective decision making are promoted throughout the project cycle – from programming through to identification, formulation, implementation and evaluation (EC 2004b).

Additionally, the guidelines provide an overall methodical and decision-making framework, which must be supported by the application of other specific "technical" and "process" tools such as the instructions found in the procurement guidelines (EC 2004b). Several persons have criticized these methods, including those interviewed in the preparation of this book who noted that the guidelines created a culture of aid dependency that resulted in implementers becoming slaves to the stipulated process, often driven by fear of breach with the ensuing penalties. The European Union has refuted these claims, noting that one of its primary mandates is to increase its support for building capacity of non-state actors as a medium for strengthening their voices in the development process and to advance political, social and economic dialogue (EC 2004a).

The guidelines are also supposed to be committed to poverty eradication, ownership, partnership, delivering more and better aid and promoting policy coherence for development. Communities in member states are guided toward a spirit of complementarity through their development cooperation activities. The European Union acknowledges that development, specifically sustainable development, is a central goal, which comprises good governance, human rights and political, economic, social and environmental development (EC 2004a).

One major challenge faced by the international community, however, is the assurance that globalization is a positive force. Poverty reduction and sustainable development promotion are objectives in their own right. The guidelines are expected to allow least developed and other low-income countries to attain more balanced global development while recognizing the value of directed individualistic aid activities. The guidelines are framed to work with all development partners to increase the quality and impact of the European Union's aid as well as to improve donor practices. In summary, the European Union will implement and monitor its commitments on aid effectiveness in developing countries while the guidelines also assist the European Union action for development, which is central to the eradication of poverty in the context of sustainable development (EC 2004b).

The Development Agenda

In many countries around the world, the EU PCM is one of the benchmarking tools for the implementation and measurement of project success (Mosse 1996). Indeed, local EU project practitioners see this text as critical to the development agenda. However, the step-by-step approach it presents can be viewed as both superficial and complex. Accordingly, arguments as presented throughout this book are grounded in the history of international development assistance, particularly as it relates to "texts" that guide development outcomes, and which have been problematized around the world (Nascimento 2017). These development challenges are evident when we compare, for example, Rostow's (1960) *Stages of Economic Growth*, which is a non-communist manifesto, to the current International Monetary Fund (IMF) agreements that impact several countries around the world (Nascimento 2017). Based on the history of development management, an in-depth holistic deconstruction of the true nature and inner workings of the discourses of this text is necessary, as no study to date has been undertaken to critique the discursive influence of the EU PCM. Therefore, an examination becomes necessary not only to fill the intellectual gap in the literature on project management but also to contribute to successful project outcomes that translate into community empowerment and national development. This book fills that gap and strengthens the possibilities for successful project outcomes.

The guidelines are not the first of its kind. The standards have been applied in Jamaica and many other underdeveloped and developing countries, which have been beneficiaries of these varied "texts of development". Other texts of development or guidelines include those from the United States through the USAID; the World Bank, the Inter-American Development Bank and the United Nations (UN). However, although numerous, these texts have not engendered the type of guaranteed development that they have promised.

In Jamaica, instead of the anticipated reduction in crime and poverty, the intent of a number of these intervention programmes, the result has been a shift in crime from one area to others, particularly those that are more urban, thus producing higher rates of violence. For example, crime, poverty and lack of education are still persistent cries from the Jamaican landscape. Kingston, the capital city of Jamaica, has historically been recording higher rates of violence, with murder rates reaching 96.2 per 100,000 in 2008, and crime rates in some areas of the city as high as 1,000 per 100,000 (Ministry of National Security and Justice [MNSJ] 2013). According to the MNSJ (2017), 7,220 acts of crime were reported in 2015. A qualitative survey of the youth situation noted that "beyond deaths, millions more children, women and men suffer from the far-reaching consequences of violence in our homes, schools and communities" (NCYD 2013, 17). The Economic and Social Survey of Jamaica (PIOJ 2016) also reported that a large majority of the labour force (66.9 per cent) has no formal training, with youth unemployment at a high of 13.5 per cent (females were 17.8 per cent; males were 9.9 per cent). Unemployment rates remained higher among females despite notable improvement in educational attainment and delayed childbearing. The minimum wage is currently J$5,600.00 for a 40-hour week with special rates for security guards at J$8,198.80 (PIOJ 2016).

Through the Department for International Development (DFID) and the 9th European Development Fund, the EU financed the Poverty Reduction Programme II (PRP II) in collaboration with the Government of Jamaica (GOJ), over a five-year implementation period from 2007 to 2013. This followed the Poverty Reduction Programme I, which focused mainly on improvement of infrastructure within communities in the areas of health, sanitation, roads and education (EC 2004b). The participatory approach to development in PRP II focused primarily on building the capacity of communities through a community-based contracting (CBC) system, where community-based groups were trained to undertake the procurement of goods and services and implement the projects while the Jamaica Social Investment Fund (JSIF) played a facilitatory role (EC 2004a). In an effort to encourage the successful implementation of the project, the programme partnered with several Jamaican agents, such as the JSIF, the MNSJ and the Social Development Commission (SDC) (EC 2004a).

The discourses surrounding the guidelines focus on promoting consistency and clarity of approach, while allowing for the operational flexibility required for a dynamic and diverse external assistance programme. The EU PRP II guidelines are also viewed as a co-operative partnership exercise between donors and recipients (EC 2004a), although this book will argue against this premise. It is stated that developing countries are accountable for their own advancement, and development assistance can only be secondary and complementary to these countries' own efforts (DAC 1996). However, project performance relies on donor and recipient accomplishment because both have an interest in, and responsibility for, the best use of scarce resources.

This book critically analyses the discourse existent with the use of the EU PCM guidelines as the prescribed text for the successful development, conceptualization, management and implementation of social development projects administered in Jamaica. More specifically, it examines the discourse that existed during the planning, implementation and evaluation stage of the JSIF PRP II project in an attempt to understand the discourses within the guidelines established for development by the EU PCM and determine how and in what ways these discourses have influenced the management and outcomes of the EU PRP II development projects such as those facilitated by JSIF.

Jamaica Social Investment Fund

Established in 1996 as a component of the GOJ's national poverty alleviation strategy, the JSIF is a limited liability company primarily funded by a loan negotiated between the GOJ and the World Bank (EC 2004a). Its lifespan was initially four years, although it has been in operation for over eighteen years with a mandate to continue until 2020 (JSIF 2006). This mandate was mainly to channel resources to small-scaled community-based projects (EC 2004a). The JSIF is governed by a board of directors whose eleven members are representative of a wide cross section of the Jamaican society. It oversees several activities such as projects, finance and audit, and procurement and contracts. The operations manual functions as a guide to ensure transparency, accountability and efficiency in project implementation (JSIF 2006).

The primary goal of the JSIF is to encourage mobilization of resources that are then channelled into the community-based socio-economic infrastructure and social services projects to empower communities and develop national capacity so as to effectively and efficiently implement community-based programmes aimed at social development (JSIF 2006).

JSIF EU PRP II Development Project

The JSIF PRP II was sponsored by the European Union under the 9th European Development Fund and the GOJ over a period of five years starting in 2007 (EC 2004a). The programme was valued at €11.6 million and saw collaboration between the JSIF and two other major agencies. The main activities were socio-economic projects concentrating on civil works, with additional social measures within unstable and vulnerable communities through capacity building and training for communities by the Ministry of National Security. Another component of the programme was the strengthening of organizations through strengthening of the Social Development Commission (SDC) (EC 2004a).

Twenty-five civil works projects in volatile communities were approved for funding at an estimated J$510 million. The list of recipients by parish were:

Clarendon: Effortville Basic School Construction, Effortville; Effortville Primary School Rehabilitation, Effortville; Hazard Primary School and Special Education Unit Rehabilitation, Canaan Heights.

Kingston: Allman Town Infant School, Allman Town; Allman Town Primary School, Allman Town; Harbour Road Rehabilitation, Rockfort; Windward Road Primary and Junior High School Expansion and Reha-bilitation, Rockfort; Tiverton Road, Rockfort; Rusden Road, Rockfort.

St Andrew: Constant Spring Primary and Junior High School Expansion and Rehabilitation, Cassava Piece; Melrose Primary and Junior High School Rehabilitation, Kencot; Maverley Primary and Junior High School Expan-sion, Maverley; Jarrett Lane Road Upgrading, Mountain View; Tower Hill Missionary Early Childhood Institute, Tower Hill; End Time Basic School Construction, Waterhouse; St Patrick's Primary School, Waterhouse; Maranatha Ministries Basic School Construction, Waterhouse.

St Catherine: St Monica's Home for the Aged Fencing, Central Village; Gregory Park Primary School Fencing, Rehabilitation and Expansion, Gregory Park; Homestead Community Centre, Homestead; March Pen Community Centre Upgrade – Multipurpose Court and Football Field,

March Pen; Newlands Basic School Expansion, Newlands; New Horizons
Skills Training Centre, Wynter's Pen; Spanish Town.

St James: Albion Basic School Construction, Albion; Glendevon Primary
and Junior High School Rehabilitation, Glendevon; Call to Excellence
Basic School Rehabilitation and Equipping, Norwood; the works to
Maverley Primary and Junior High, and Jarrett Lane Road Upgrading.
(EC 2010)

Six grants, each under €10,000 for community-related activities, were also
awarded. These focused on youth development, including training and internships, parenting skills training, and tertiary education scholarships. Additionally, the Lucea Family Courthouse was constructed and furnished (EC 2004a).

As mentioned earlier, the EU PCM presents another attempt in a long line
of texts of development. Thus, the overarching objective of this book is to
critically analyse the discourse existent with the use of the EU PCM guidelines as the prescribed text for the successful development, conceptualization,
management and implementation of social development projects administered
in Jamaica. More specifically, the study examines the discourse that existed
during the planning, implementation and evaluation stage of the JSIF PRP II
project. Accordingly, the primary objectives of the book are to understand the
discourses of the EU project management for development guidelines and
determine how and in what ways these discourses have influenced the management and outcomes of EU PRP II development projects such as those implemented by JSIF.

Understanding Discourse Analysis

Critical discourse analysis is used as a methodological and interpretive framework in the conduct of this study. Discourse analysis is a broad and diverse
field, inclusive of various approaches in understanding the phenomena of
language and text while utilizing various analytical practices (Wetherell, Taylor
and Yates 2001). When defined as systems of meaning, discourses are influenced by interactional and sociocultural context and operate through written
or spoken languages (Wetherell, Taylor and Yates 2001). These forms operate
conjointly with vocal and visual elements in the context of meaning-laden
architectures (Fairclough et al. 2004).

A key element to discourse analysis is its ability to examine language through
careful scrutiny of the ways in which reality and experiences are constructed
through social and interpersonal processes. A critical component of this is
the reflexive process, which this author observed through the method of

bracketing. The discourse was done by investigating (1) the various definitions presented for development and the different contributors to the development discourse; (2) the negotiation of agencies, responsibilities and the dynamics that existed between donors, implementers and beneficiaries of the projects; (3) the role of the guidelines in shaping the outcomes and impacts of the projects and their ability to reduce poverty and crime in order for development to be achieved; (4) the use of power and resistance and how these have translated into impacting the development agenda; and (5) the role of hegemonic discourses in shaping problems faced by beneficiaries of the programme and the proposed solutions (Avdi and Georgaca 2009).

Fairclough (2003) argued that discourse is no longer preoccupied with the analysis of the text but instead focused more on systems and regulations that govern bodies of the text, and the processes that the texts themselves govern dialectically. Accordingly, discourses categorized and no longer simply described the social world but also entailed subject positions, which the speaker adopted when employing language. This was important to note because this had fundamental consequences both for the sense of self and experience of the implementers of the project, the actions they were allowed to take and the duties they were expected to perform to ensure the reliability and validity of the data.

Second, there is a mutual relationship between discourses and institutions. Discourses are shaped and distributed through institutional practices, which in turn authenticate and maintain these practices through language and text.

Finally, discourse and power are heavily intertwined. This is evident based on the symbiotic nature of the relationship as the owners of power make accessible varied forms of reality and personhood, while marginalizing other knowledges and associated practices. The ability of a discourse to influence social practice or the reverse is reliant on power dynamics. Harvey (1996) argued that in such instances, discourses often crystallize into "things", "elements", and "insoluble domains" or "systems" that assume a relative permanence contained by a social system and/or among other discourses. Based on these power dynamics, some discourses can, for example, hierarchically position themselves above other discourses. Also, as Titscher et al. (2000) argued, power relations can play a critical role in discourse as they influence society and culture. Society and culture are designed by, and at the same time establish, discourse (Harvey 1996). This was achieved after the exploration of discourse analysis in talks of infiltration and other kinds of texts. This approach involved examination of the effects of the guidelines on project implementers, the experiences of beneficiaries and engagement of all stakeholders. These formulated discourses reproduced and challenged culturally dominant ways to understand the communities, institutions and the social order that existed.

A simple area for discourse analysis relates to the practical aspect of language. Consequently, the first step in the analysis was to observe the ways in which the objects under study were created in the guidelines. In discourse analysis, language is evaluated in terms of structure and purpose. Language is also measured as a form of social action. Aid donors used language to achieve certain development goals. Discourse analysis evaluates how subjects are created based on people's recollection and the inconsistency in these events and explores the rhetoric components and the purposes of talk in the context of development (Potter 2003).

The second level of analysis evaluates the changing aspects of interaction between development discourse and the use of language and text. This was the approach with which participants used language and managed the interactions. Here, the author examined the feedback from all stakeholders involved in the implementation of the project and the rhetorical strategies used by the researcher in order to present a credible, objective, reliable and rational evaluation of the project. In terms of examining the function of talk, the author examined the speaker's utterance in relation to the discourse in which it was produced and further explored its origin and what pre-existed.

This is a unique approach to project evaluation that has not been undertaken in international project management for international development assistance. By focusing on discourse, we are able to unearth substantive characteristics of events, objects, subjects, structures, phenomena, and so on (Fairclough 2003). By using critical discourse analysis as a methodological and interpretive framework, unacknowledged aspects of human behaviour were revealed that aided in the success or hindrance of projects and the positions held by each stakeholder. The technique also helped to identify and develop a variety of new and alternative social subject's positions projected to empower beneficiary communities and their residents if utilized during project delivery. Understanding the meaning of language and discourse also promotes positive individual and social change because it presents a critical challenge to traditional theory, policy and practice. Therefore, the use of a reflective stance was incorporated to facilitate the adoption of neutrality.

Based on all this, the writer questioned the following:

1. What are the discourses of the EU PCM (the guidelines)?
2. How and in what ways have these discourses influenced the outcomes of EU PRP II development projects at JSIF? and
3. To what extent do the EU PRP II development project guidelines represent a tool for the continuation of Western-Northern hegemony?

The Significance of the Study

The study upon which this book is based is pivotal in shaping our understanding of the current discourse on development and how current structural changes can benefit underprivileged communities, by contributing to the goals of Jamaica's Vision 2030. One way of achieving this is through proper management of social development intervention projects that are driven by the needs of the beneficiaries. The acknowledgment and establishment of partnerships are also needed to foster community development (UN 2015).

An examination of the literature through an academic lens highlights a deficit. Authors often discuss development in a vacuum, failing to advance a contemporary development-thinking standpoint with specific reference to a local phenomenon (UN 2011). This book therefore provides a critique toward alternative and multiple ways of framing the development problem from a local standpoint, with reference to the EU PCM system, the prescribed development text. This examination of the discourse is expected to lead to community development and empowerment of individuals by elevating the capacity of all stakeholders engaged in the project. The development narrative is further expanded to incorporate processes, project implementers and social institutions seen as equitable partners. These attributes are important both to international relations and to the development conversation.

The study is also unique because it reflects the Jamaican reality and by extension, that of the Caribbean. Most case studies are of Africa and Asia, giving the erroneous impression that little research is conducted in the Caribbean region. The study also contributes to the Jamaican development agenda, which is centred on utilizing our limited resources to achieve greater development through the creation of more impactful and sustainable projects that will lead to greater capacity development as community members are given voices.

Theoretical Framework

The theoretical framework was used as a medium for supporting and conducting the study because it helped shape the research perspective, underscoring that the investigation is not based on personal instincts but rather established theory and empirical facts (Simon and Goes 2011).

The theoretical framework connects the researcher to previous knowledge and is guided by relevant theories based on the research questions and methodology. The theoretical assumptions address questions of why and how to transition from simply describing the observed phenomenon, to making generalizations. The primary reason for having theories is to identify limits to these generalizations.

Post-development Theory

Post-development authors regard development as an extension of colonialism (Rahnema 1997). The foundation of post-development theory is that development, the discourse and its goals have not worked and so shortcomings are criticized in post-development texts. For example, Ziai (2004) noted that post-development offered alternatives in its formation of communal solidarity, direct democracy, social movements, indigenous and traditional knowledge. Earlier, Nustad (2001, 22) observed that development was often seen "as a means and a goal". Based on the development narrative presented by previous post-development authors such as Rahnema (1997) and Escobar (1997), the implication is that the goal is present at the onset of the development process, therefore creating the perception that those who are to be "developed" desire it. This alludes to the bottoms-up approach to development that would mean confusing the means and goals of development (Nustad 2001). Ziai (2004) also raised concerns where development projects use participatory processes and the community to be developed chose not to be changed as an option. If this was accepted based on existing discourse, it would negate the argument presented for development to be regarded as a means and goal.

Post-development authors argue that the goal toward social change cannot be legitimately defined by an outside expert, a fact that this study has confirmed. The decision to change must be the remit of target actors who have the right to decide their own development agenda (Ziai 2004). Escobar (2006) examined the development pervasive cultural discourse by exploring the failures and limitations of the state, market and international aid to a form of social change. This is led by new social movements and progressive non-governmental organizations that address the relationship that exists between donors and beneficiary communities. Also, examined throughout the process was the discourse of power and control as presented by Escobar, for whom development discourse is not neutral knowledge, and has normalizing effects. What is seen to be a neutral response has translated into a practical problem.

The post-development theoretical approach also complements critical discourse analysis as the methodological approach applied to development. Pieterse (2000) noted that post-development use of discourse analysis is an ideological platform rooted in the Foucauldian approach. It is not about the veracity of developmental discourse but how historically the discourse has produced the effect of being the truth (Pieterse 2000; Storey 2000). For post-development theorists, the failure of development to reduce poverty or to discipline or dominate is not the central problem of the developmental discourse. This has therefore resulted in communities that benefit from aid development projects remaining objectified (Storey 2000). Lastly, these alternatives to development come from the development of beneficiaries of aid. It is because of these development weaknesses that the post-development interpretation of the relations of power and knowledge of the discourse has impacted to the rejection of development (Pieterse 2000, 2001; Ziai 2004).

Western-Northern Hegemony

The term Western-Northern hegemony is critical to the development discourse because it highlights the domination of developed over developing countries. A hegemonic system is created when one nation-state achieves greater economic power and convinces subordinate states that it is in their best interest to accept the leadership of the dominant power. This hegemonic ideology promotes the national and collective interest of the funding country. Throughout this book, Western-Northern hegemony is discussed from a political standpoint. This view enables superpowers to dominate and dictate project terms, usually attained through the active consent of countries in receipt of grant funding for development projects or interventions.

Understanding global and regional power relationships is critical to development discourse, and the considered influence of strategic political factors, for example, controlling global money circulation and determining the international agenda, are all critical elements in the Western hegemonic relationship. Volgy, Frazier and Ingersoll (2003) classified hegemony as having the ability and influence to transform the rules and norms of international systems based on impetus and aspiration. The trio also explored this position of power and noted that a hegemonic relationship is based on two kinds of strength: relational and structural. Relation-based power is the ability to persuade and encourage other actors, while structural power is the essential capacity to realize desired rules, norms and operations in the international system (Volgy, Frazier and Ingersoll 2003).

The Western-Northern hegemony is not based solely on consent, but also entails a certain amount of coercion. Consent is a key component to understanding how hegemony is established and upheld. Developing countries of the South, when faced with challenges, are often forced to accept prescribed guidelines and will consent and submit to the hegemonic power of the Western North. The hegemon provides a sense of security, sovereignty, as well as prosperity. The narrative around hegemony contributes to a better understanding when examining intervention programmes. Barrett (1997) also contributed to this concept because he suggested power was not only dependent on force but also on consent. Nye (2002) believed that hegemonic power by persuasion would ensure better utilization of soft power that made other countries believe in common interests.

Tools of Western-Northern Hegemony

Hegemonic apparatuses are formal or informal tools commonly employed by Western-Northern institutions. They consist of autonomous rules, norms, procedures and guidelines (Heywood 2007), and are critical for the establishment and coordination of expectations of project activities between countries with the intent to minimize conflict. Hegemonic apparatuses produce social and political systems that are then applied to the targeted country. A hegemonic nation creates or maintains key regimes to reduce uncertainty. This is achieved through "open and active power" that is usually applied to impact the attitude of another country. Additionally, covert power, thought to be a passive approach, is another tool used by Western hegemonic countries but when organized and utilized is an effective way of setting agendas.

Brzezinski (2004) claims that structural power, possessed by some nations, is dependent on three elements in international political economy. These are: maintaining the control of goods and service production systems; maintaining the authority of determination and management possibilities in finance and credit institutions; and retaining the most effective instruments to influence knowledge and information through acquiring, production and communication.

Methodology

Critical discourse analysis, data collection and analysis, and sampling techniques, along with emancipatory and critical research design, have been used in the preparation of this book. Because of its ability to provide detailed information, a qualitative framework was the main medium employed for data collection, which allowed for a comprehensive description of the discourse surrounding the EU PCM guidelines. It was also important because it addressed the social realities concerning the use of the text in the implementation of the JSIF PRP II project.

The main purpose of embarking on emancipatory qualitative research was to emphasize the following: (1) all relationships are highlighted in the involvement of the imbalance of power and (2) the participants themselves are the best experts on their life situations, therefore the best persons to assess the benefits or weaknesses of the guidelines.

Critical discourse analysis is used to unpack the development discourse. Development is often seen as multidimensional, and is influenced by various definitions and expectations prejudiced by cultural and social discourses. Critical discourse analysis is a multilevel approach, comprising different perspectives for reviewing the relationship between the use of language and social context. Critical discourse analysis also focuses on the cultural and economic dimensions as substantial in the development and maintenance of power relations (Fairclough 2000, 2001, 2003; van Dijk 2001; Wodak 2001).

It has the ability to address social problems, focuses on the linguistic characteristics of social and cultural processes and facilitates the exploration of these by being better able to understand explicit power relationships that are frequently hidden. The primary aim was to derive the contexts for social, cultural, political and even economic results (Fairclough and Wodak 1997). The second principle is that power relations are discursive. The critical discourse analysis approach clarifies how social relations of power are implemented and converted in and through discourse (Fairclough and Wodak 1997), which was needed to allow general inferences to be made based on the current social and cultural realities. The author also utilized this technique to identify problems and make recommendations based on the power dynamics, interpretative and explanatory in approach and intent (Fairclough 2001), which are dynamic and open, and affected by several factors such as readings and contextual information.

The evaluation of texts was also used in linguistics, semiotic, literary analysis and the macro-analysis of social formations, institutions, and power relations that influenced them (Luke 2002). Therefore, an understanding of the guidelines was important. Understanding the context in which it was written and identifying the intended audience was crucial in shaping our understanding of the text. Fairclough (1995) referred to this as the multi-semiotic character that written or spoken language produces in a discursive event.

Genre was another key area of focus for development discourse. Fairclough defined it as "the use of language associated with a particular social activity" (1993, 138). Different genres represent means of production of "specifically textual sort, different resources for texturing" (Fairclough 2000, 12). This refers to a form of textual structuring based on a set of relatively stable conventions, which are both creative and conservative and explores whether the approach is relatively stable and at the same time open to change after examination. One of the findings of the study was based on the inflexible and cumbersome nature of the written text when implementing social development projects, influenced by attempts to maintain good governance structures while eliminating pockets of corruption. However, the rigidness presented several challenges that influenced the impact of the projects.

Another approach utilized was intertextuality and interdiscursivity as part of the methodological technique used in unpacking the development discourse. The notion of intertextuality offers a perspective of both reading and writing texts as a way of looking at a text's interactions with the intended audience, writers and other documents. Fairclough explained this perspective stating, "all texts, spoken and written, are constructed and have the meanings which text-users assign to them in and through their relations with other texts in some social formation" (2003, 45). Intertextuality and intertextual analysis in this book facilitated the unpacking of the discourse surrounding the use of the guidelines and also provided a linguistic analysis of the text (Fairclough 2003). According to Fairclough (1995), intertextual analysis focused on the marginal line between text and discourse practice in the analytical framework. Conversely, interdiscursivity is an amalgamation of genres and discourses in the text and the prevalence in, and the control of political, ideological and cultural domains of a society (Fairclough 2003). Fairclough also attributed three dimensions to each discursive event. To achieve this, the author also benefited from several interviews, focus groups and document analysis that helped to highlight a number of the conclusions drawn for the study.

Summary

This book demonstrates the examination of the discourse based on Fairclough's three analysis components: description, interpretation and explanation. Linguistic properties of texts are explained using text analysis to ascertain the association between the productive and interpretative methods of discursive practice and the text (Fairclough 2003). This is then interpreted, the relationship between discursive practice and social practice is explained, and inferences are made that suggest recommendations that can aid in the manifestation of development and community empowerment.

2.

A Critique of Development

Post-development theory emerged in the 1980s as scholars and activists expressed dissatisfaction with the concept and practice of *development*. Inspired by the works of philosophers and activists such as Illich, Foucault, Gandhi, Polanyi and others, Escobar (1995, 1996), Esteva and Prakash (1998), Rahnema (1997) and Latouche (1989) worked together to yield the first among three major works most often understood as representative of post-development theory (Ziai 2007). This era of development signalled a process of providing opportunities for most of the developing world and broadening of the gap between rich and poor countries. Authors concluded that development was a misguided initiative because it indirectly intended to eliminate cultural diversity through the universalizing of Western institutions. The development discourse shaped an incompetent apparatus for producing information about, and the exercise of power over, the Third World (Escobar 1995).

Post-development articulated a dissatisfaction with the concept and practice of the term "development" that led not to the search for alternative versions but to the dismissal of it altogether and a call for alternatives (Esteva and Prakash 1998; Escobar 1995; Rahnema 1997). There were some fundamental problems with the way development has been pursued in the post–World War II era. This was articulated after examination of the prescriptions advanced to bridge the development gap, in spite of critics' claim of the opposite – that post-development can inform practice and reveal the direction of potential alternatives. Post-development has its roots in postmodern critique of modernity. Attempts at deconstructing the concept of development were undertaken (Escobar 1995) in order to reveal the operations of power and knowledge in development discourse and practices. Post-development writers sought to dismiss the World War II concept of developing by referring to the top-down authoritarian form, as directed by intrusive state mechanisms and international development.

The Evolution of Development

At the end of 1945, underdevelopment in some countries became synonymous with terms like poverty, inadequate technology and capital, rapid population growth and insufficient public services. Other terms introduced with more caution or in an underhanded way included cultural attitudes and values, and the existence of racial, religious, geographic or ethnic factors believed to be associated with backwardness (Cowen and Shenton 1996). Ethnicity and ethnocentrism were thought to have influenced a new form of development, while indigenous populations were earmarked for modernization where the concept meant the adoption of the "right" values, that is, the preconceived ideologies of what were considered markers of development (Kanstrup-Jensen 2006). Thus, forms of power in terms of class, gender, race and nationality found their way into development theory and practice creating the formative elements of the development discourse. Development in Europe focused on reconstruction and rapid economic growth, while in Africa they were more focused on "post-colonial development" (Ziai 2007, 11).

This ideology, whether in its more extreme articulations or in the more nuanced discourses of modernization and development, is a dangerous one (Munck and O'Hearn 1999). The strengths and weaknesses of development thinking are its policy-oriented character that forms part of its vitality and inventiveness. It is problem-driven rather than theory-driven, worldly grounded, and street-smart driven by field knowledge. This, therefore, rendered development theories non-existent in the field of social sciences. This can be seen in the inability to clearly establish a working and agreeable definition that overarches all the elements of the social sciences. Despite this, dependency theory is heavily influenced by the nuances of development theory.

The core meaning of development was economic growth as well as growth theory. Development acts as a reflection of shifting economic and social capacities, significances and choice by naming these as the North and South geographical conceptions of the world (Haferkamp and Smeleser 1992). These geographical thoughts (Gregory 1998) are impacting policy decision and action. This approach describes the role of creating discourses that accept some meanings of development as truth, such as modernization, and other definitions as false, such as dependency (Foucault 1980; Escobar 1997). This network of presumed international agencies has the power of identifying what they agree is the predominant discourse. These discourses are taken as the unchallengeable truth and anyone with conflicting thoughts is marginalized (Rostow 1960). An example of this truth as a source of marginalization is seen in the whole-hearted use of the EU guidelines, accepted by countries worldwide as one of the primary templates for ensuring the success and advancement of development projects.

Additionally, to understand the development discourse and how it operates, one must look at the system of relations established among these institutions and practices, and the systematization of these relations to form a whole that speaks to the objects, concepts, theories and strategies needed for the discourse (Escobar 1995). Escobar viewed development as "a mode of thinking and a source of practices, [which have] become an omnipresent reality. As poor countries became the target of a number of programs and interventions that ensured their control" (378).

First, the traditional concept of development is seen as a Eurocentric construct where the West is labelled "developed" and the rest of the world is perceived as "underdeveloped". This constitutes one society as the ideal and others as deviations from that norm while neglecting numerous other possible conceptions and indicators for a good life or a good society, since the different ways of measuring development are modelled upon the European experience of progress. According to post-development theory, these values of development should not be taken as universal (Ziai 2007). Second, it is argued that the traditional concept of development has authoritarian and technocratic implications. Whoever gets to decide what development is and how it can be achieved, is usually called a development expert, and assumes a position of power that has been described as a trusteeship. Post-development thinkers such as Ziai (2007) observed that political power in the hands of persons who believed the world to be homogeneous held the danger of the ascription of a generic standard to classify and evaluate societies. The key to post-development arguments is that development discourse is grounded in Western ideas of progress and as such takes the form of an imposition of those ideas on the South, thereby repressing local cultures and interests (Parfitt 2002).

Furthermore, the production of knowledge is one of the ways in which the West controls and even creates the Third World politically, economically, culturally and sociologically. Under the rubric of modernization, development is postulated as a natural process (Munck and O'Hearn 1999). This process is needed to create the imagery of a dependency relationship between developed and underdeveloped countries, assigning the former the role of saviour, rescuing the less developed population from misery, disease and stagnation thanks to advanced technology. At the deepest level, however, roles may have to be reversed. Perhaps it is developed nations that must be saved from servitude by means of creative options yet to be made in underdeveloped societies as they struggle to modernize in a human mode (Denis 1977).

Another concept of development is human development. Human development is proposed as being much deeper, richer and more critical to the development process, with the ability to present a clearer picture of what constitutes development than that which is captured by any complex index or even by a full set of statistical indicators. It is useful to streamline a complex reality because that is the primary mandate of the Human Development Index (Bakker and

Leisinger 2013). The Human Development Index is a composite index of achievements in basic human capabilities in three fundamental dimensions – a long and healthy life, knowledge and a decent standard of living – thus recognizing that economic growth is not the end of development or the medium of assessing developmental success. It also highlights the need to encompass not only economic factors, but also the environment, politics and social welfare in a balanced perspective on development (UNDP 2010). Therefore, to understand development as a discourse, one must look not at the elements themselves but at the system of relations established among them.

Sen (1999) also contended that development of freedom is both the primary end and the principal means of development. Presenting development as a multidimensional process therefore does not admit to any one form of measurement. In the 1980s, the World Bank endorsed economic growth as the goal of development. It declared this in its 1991 *World Development Report*, using rarely heard normative language.

Post-development assessment of development by writers such as Ferguson (1990) and Escobar (1995) were impacted by scholarly traditions of Marx and Foucault. They saw development discourse as a tool of surveillance and control. In order to preserve a focus on the notion of power and domination, as well as on the most persistent effects of development, they saw development in terms of discourse. Escobar saw development from a discourse analysis perspective as he perceived development as a historically shaped discourse that entailed an examination of discovering why so many countries began to see themselves as underdeveloped in the early post–World War II period. Their fundamental problem became how "to develop" and how to embark upon the task of underdeveloping themselves by subjecting their societies to increasingly systematic, detailed and comprehensive interventions (Escobar 1995).

Escobar also outlined how the discourse on the Third World was constructed in the development discourse as poverty being highlighted and problematized. He claimed two-thirds of the world's population was subjected to these discursive practices as, "The poor gradually was seen as a social problem needing an original way of intervention in society, and the treatment of poverty allowed society to conquer new domains" (2000, 22). The management of poverty called for an involvement in areas such as education, health, hygiene, morality and employment, as well as inculcating good socialization and fiscal behaviours. The result was a display of interventions that accounted for the domain of knowledge and innovation. Other factors were singled out as social problems to include health, education, hygiene, employment and citizens' quality of life. Rehabilitation would require widespread knowledge about the population and suitable modes of social planning (Escobar 1992). The Third World was rebranded as an inferior and negative concept, which was concretized by estab-lishing its distance from the more civilized and developed West. The construct laid the foundation for curative treatment and interventions that were covert and sophisticated. Escobar saw the rich countries of the West "creating an extremely efficient tool for producing knowledge about, and exercise of power over, the Third World" (1995, 3).

Also, the poor's ability to define and manage their lives was further under-mined. They became test subjects for the West's sophisticated programming of interventions. Development issues depended on precise relations recognized in the midst of discourse relations between the recommendations of experts and international funders. And so, the term "development" was considered not as a cultural process but as an organization generally applicable with tech-nical interventions intended to distribute needed goods to a target population (Castro 2004). The invention of development forged an institutional field from which discourses were produced, recorded, stabilized, modified and circulated. As a result, social life was conceived as a technical problem whose team of professionals were the only ones qualified to deliver rational and managerial decisions (Castro 2004).

Interestingly, development practice is not static. The construct was purposed to be about the citizens caught in the maelstrom; instead, development wound up as an autocratic, ethnocentric and technocratic approach that treated people and cultures as abstract concepts fluctuating on statistical charts (Escobar 1995). Development became paramount for Third World countries so much so that rulers subjected their nationals to an unending slew of interventions, thus reinforcing power and systems of control. Interventions were so important that elites from developed nations actively participated by endorsing underdevel-opment, sale of national assets, degradation of physical and human geologies, carnage and torture, and extermination of indigenous populations, so that Third World citizens developed such low esteem that they bought into the idea of reason and progress (Escobar 1995).

Development was conceived as a system of universally applicable technical interventions intended to efficiently deliver desirable goods to a target popula-tion. This meant, therefore, that development became a destructive force to Third World cultures under the guise of the people's interests (Escobar 1995).

Post-development: A Call for Change

The fundamental post-development position arguably shows that if authori-tarian and ethnocentric elements for development were to be avoided, it would be impossible to define development in normative terms as the state of a "good society". Such a definition could only legitimately be reached through a democratic process by the people concerned (Ziai 2004). Therefore, the post-development primary mandate is to effectively transfer power. This power defines the problems and objectives of a society by the members of the society itself, removing the authority from the hands of outside experts, which adds up to a radical democratic position (Ziai 2004).

Additionally, the call for the end of development by post-development scholars does not, according to Rahnema (1997), equate to an end of the search for new possibilities of change but rather, establishes that a change is needed at the level of the people, and that what they seek is change that will increase their cultural capacities that will permit them to be free to modify the content and rules of change according to their culturally defined aspirations. This is what makes Foucault's influence on post-development theory so critical. Development is seen as constituting a specific way of thinking about the world as it is a particular form of knowledge (Rahnema 1997). According to Foucault (1980), it does not reflect reality but instead constructs reality, and as such "it closes off alternative ways of thinking and constitutes a form of power" (Kiely 1999 cited in Storey 2000, 40). Escobar (1995) attempted to deconstruct Foucauldian development discourse to reveal Foucault's analysis of power, knowledge and discourse in relation to development. This movement would demonstrate how Western disciplinary and normalizing mechanisms have served as dominating forces that they have extended to the Third World and imbibed in the production of discourses.

Furthermore, grassroots initiatives, although still clearly limited, are significant. They provide the means for an alternative to development by means of political practice (Escobar 1992). The post-development analysis is a "recognition that existing actors and institutions must be transformed to work for different purposes" (Andreasson 2010, 10). The post-development era cannot ignore questions of the future role of the development apparatus. The institutional structures are not likely to be abandoned. Post-development theorists' critique of development thinking has been affected by social engineering and the desire to mimic the economies and societies of the developed West. This method brands it an interventionist and managerialist discipline. According to Pieterse, "It involves telling other people what to do – in the name of modernisation, nation building, progress, mobilisation, sustainable development, human rights, poverty alleviation and even empowerment and participation" (2000, 1).

Also, the consistencies of effects that the developed discourse is said to achieve are important to its success for a hegemonic form of representation. The building of the poor as universal, preconstituted subjects, is grounded on the privilege of the representatives, and the exercise of power over the Third World facilitated by the discursive homogenization (Castro 2004). Development assumes a need to reform citizens or persons of indigenous descent. However, it repeatedly reproduces the separation between reforms and those framed by keeping alive the premise of the Third World as different and inferior, with incomplete humanity in relation to the accomplished European (Castro 2004).

In addition, the emphasis on an archaeology of poverty is important (Rahnema 1997). The break in the origin and management of poverty with the appearance of capitalism in Europe, and of development in the Third World, is subsequent to the advent of development.

Rahnema (1991) described the first break in the manner of nineteenth-century systems for dealing with the poor. These had profound consequences as the treatment of poverty allowed society to conquer new domains greater than an industrial and technological emergence of capitalism and modernity. A field of knowledge and involvement of the social norms became prominent in the nineteenth century, culminating in the twentieth century with the association of the welfare state and an ensemble under the rubric of social work.

Development thinking culminated in the UN Development decade in the 1960s. It primarily originated from President Truman's 1949 Point Four Program and President Kennedy's 1961 Alliance for Progress in Latin America. The United States was at the height of its power and influence and regarded itself as both the inspiration and the policeman of the world (Munck and O'Hearn 1999). But development theory essentially should not abandon the political economy approach; it must also exceed the limitations of text-bound literacy theory and its political evasiveness of Eurocentric postmodernism (Munck and O'Hearn 1999).

Also, Pieterse (2000) and Schuurman (2000) critiqued post-development theory as flawed because it suggested no alternatives. Nustad (2001 argued that while post-development offered an interesting and convincing assessment of the development apparatus, it lacked instrumentality for development practice because it did not suggest a way forward. Brigg (2002), for instance, insisted that post-development had been unduly dismissed for lacking a programme for development and should not be limited to helping us understand why so many development efforts failed. Other post-development writers have signalled that there is a collapse of modernity that is being changed by the non-modern majorities into opportunities for regretting their own traditions, cultures, unique indigenous and non-modern arts of living and dying (Esteva and Prakash 1998). Post-development thinking is criticized for being profoundly conservative, although post-development critique arises from a radical democratic and anti-authoritarian philosophy (Pieterse 2000). However, post-development has received little attention in mainstream debates because of the number of critics that have dismissed the approach, while distracted and preoccupied with the less constructive discourse that relates to a poor use of Foucauldian analysis that is distinguishable within post-development thinking.

Post-development theorists reject any form of development that has been a response to the problematization of poverty arising from World War II, and can be seen as "an historical construct that provides a space in which poor countries are known, specified and intervened upon" (Escobar 1995, 45). A criticism of post-development scholars and their alternatives to development is that the political project of post-development has been entrusted to new social movements that are far from guaranteed to be politically progressive (Storey 2000). Post-development falls under the same heading as other postmodern theorizing since it relates to practice by denying universal normative grounds. Instead, they are left with no satisfactory basis for distinguishing emancipatory from non-emancipatory practices. This is added to the fact that post-development writers have not adequately dealt with the implications of their analysis for the practice of development.

Summary

The book provides the reader with the theoretical perspectives used when one tries to shape and understand the development discourse. By organizing the different theoretical perspectives according to particular historical events, this writer was able to demonstrate the relationship that exists based on the proposed development agenda. The main theories identified were Rostow's stages of economic growth, Escobar's critiques of the development discourse (post-development theory), and Ziai's exploration of post-development theory, practice, problems and perspectives.

3.

The EU Project Management Discourses for Development

Jamaica Social Investment Fund PRP II
Key Stakeholders

The implementation of PRP II was achieved based on the established partnership between the EU, the PIOJ, the JSIF, the SDC and the Ministry of National Security. Each of these entities also formed the general organizational structure of PRP II and has contributed to project outcomes. Additionally, each institution is guided by the EU discourse in the implementation of PRP II. Figure 3.1 showcases the various organizations and how information and expectations are transferred along with the process of reporting.

The role of each organization is as follows:

The Planning Institute of Jamaica (PIOJ): The overall responsibility of the PIOJ is the implementation of the programme as the national authorizing officer. The PIOJ is accountable for the day-to-day operations entrusted to the JSIF (EC 2004a). It is also the contracting authority for the programme. This is in accordance with guidelines of the Cotonou Agreement.

The Poverty Reduction Programme II Steering Committee: The steering committee has the executive responsibility for the PRP II implementation and was guided by the MNSJ in the process of selecting eligible communities. It determines the proper strategy for non-state actors (NSAs) and oversees all matters related to the timely achievement and objectives as stipulated in the log frame. The Committee comprises: a representative of the PIOJ; the coordinator of the National Poverty Eradication Programme; a representative of the University of the West Indies; two NSA representatives – from the Council for Voluntary Social Services and Private Sector Organisation of Jamaica; a representative of the delegation of the European Commission, a representative of the JSIF; and a representative of the Ministry of National Security (EC 2004a).

The Social Development Commission (SDC): The SDC is an agency of the Ministry of Local Government with the mandate for community

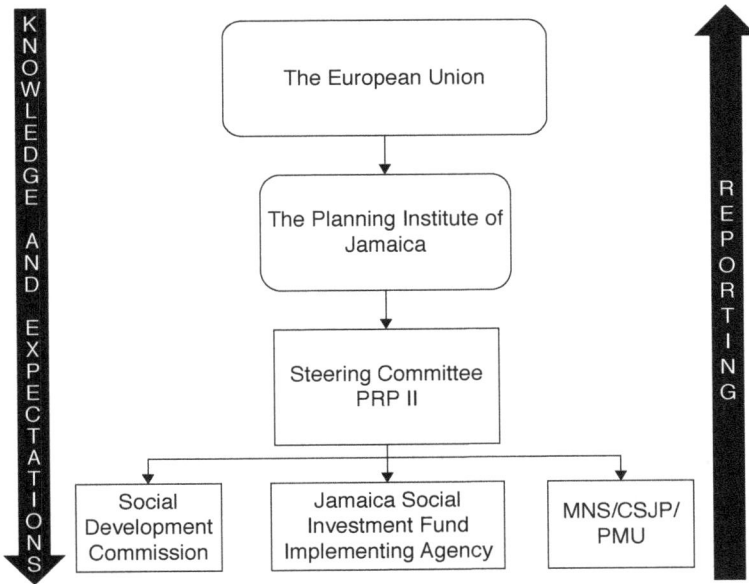

Figure 3.1. Organizational chart for PRP II

Source: Walters (2005)

development. The SDC functions as a service provider, facilitator and JSIF's primary channel to the communities (EC 2004a).

The Ministry of National Security: The primary role of the Ministry of National Security is to guide the steering committee in the process of selecting eligible volatile communities. It is also expected to create synergies between these communities, the SDC and JSIF programmes. It provides data relating to the existing projects and assists in the identification of the communities that are currently involved in crime prevention programmes (EC 2004a).

It is important to note that these stakeholders are not fixed partners and vary according to EU projects. Although partnership is a continuing theme in the rhetoric of benefactors in recent years, it has become particularly evident, because this phenomenon relates to aid policies such as improved assistance between major donors, that there is a transformed attention to areas of policy and governance on their part, and a widening of the scope of conditionalities.

Role of Key Stakeholders

The reality of aid is dependent on the role of all stakeholders. One of the factors for this is that donors influence the knowledgeable and established framework within which developing countries may choose their policies. As posited, the countries are in the driving seat but the donors retain the road map (Randel, German and Ewing 2002). Also, the financial power of donors has improved due to closer cooperation between them. The EU aid policy had always been disjointed with precise structures and procedures for different areas, and the institutional structure has changed over the years as the European Union itself and its role in the world has developed (EC 2004a).

Who has the power and can this power be challenged? These are critical questions that need to be asked when examining stakeholders' discourse. The power relationships consequently hinge on several factors that differ from project to project. The receiver's negotiating position is dependent on its geopolitical and geo-economic position, and its economic circumstances including debt and trade dependence (Girvan 2007). However, governments can increase their negotiation strength through internal organization and pledges to their sovereignty in the administration of the aid relationship – including a willingness to reject aid where the circumstances are unsuited to indigenous needs. Social consensus and political maintenance of the nego- tiating position of the recipient government is another important element. These factors indicate to the donor that a different administration is unlikely to accept a different position, while an agreement based on the current government's position is likely to be accepted (Girvan 2007). However, according to Foucault, contesting power is not a matter of searching for some absolute truth and power (Foucault 1980 quoted in Rabinow 1991, 75). An examination of the discourse is needed because discourse conveys and produces "power, reinforces it but also challenges and exposes it, rendering it delicate and makes it possible to prevent" (Foucault 1998, 95). This is another approach of critiquing this module and text for development as Foucault's approach has been widely used to critique development thinking and para- digms, and the ways in which development discourses are saturated with power (Gaventa 2003).

From the data collected, a critical component for the implementation of PRP II was the establishment of a collaborative effort and established partner- ship between the EU, the PIOJ, the JSIF, the SDC and the MNSJ. The concept of partnership is not new to the literature with regard to project success and aid donors. The term implies a supportive relationship based on the philoso- phies of mutuality and equality. However, this was not the case in the imple- mentation of PRP II because the European Union, as funder of the project, is positioned at the top level followed by the PIOJ, the Steering Committee, the MNSJ, the Community Safety Security and Justice Programme (CSJP), JSIF and the SDC.

Neither the SDC nor the MNSJ felt like equal partners in the implementation of the project. Instead, similar sentiments were echoed during the elite interviews from MNSJ and SDC representatives:

> The report is there; and from a SDC position, again, the main thing is the lack of communication to SDC and primarily the absence of SDC from that dialogue; and we were expected to bring that into PRP II and ensure that the communities were represented and that their views and work on the projects [emanated] from the ground up. . . . Similar gaps were faced in PRP I and recommendations made to make SDC more of an equal partner. But unfortunately that did not happen for PRP II. (Respondent SDC, 6 March 2014)

This implies that the established partnership between the SDC and JSIF needs to be strengthened and better communication needs to be had between the European Union and the SDC. Representatives from CSJP and MNSJ also felt that the level of (EU) engagement with JSIF should be extended to all stakeholders.

Jamaica Social Investment Fund

The JSIF is the implementing agency for the PRP II. Its primary responsibility includes coordination and monitoring of the programme. It is tasked with the coordination of sub-projects through JSIF technical and administrative structures under the supervision of the steering committee (EC 2004a).

Another element in the discourse structure is JSIF's role in the implementation of PRP II as an implementing agency, a critical component, where project objectives and expectations are communicated by the European Union and translated into outputs. The project implementation may be seen as putting into action the activities of the project, along with that which was proposed in the programme estimate, financial agreement and the overall intention regarding the management of the project. The JSIF has managed to successfully implement projects with the assistance of government support from agencies such as the PIOJ and SDC. This has helped with the attainment of the project's objectives, through the allocation of knowledge, human and financial resources and administrative support. In addition, the guidelines presented by the European Union are very detailed and provide JSIF with the support needed for successful implementation. Careful management of time and resources and the oversight of good managers – sound project management – are key to project success. However, there is no simple formula for the successful implementation of the EU PRP II project. Instead, at its heart, what is required for success is effective project planning, design and implementation.

Several concerns were raised by organizations such as the SDC with regard to JSIF's ability to successfully implement the projects' objectives based on their reach and capacity, because SDC representatives interviewed felt that they had greater reach and flexibility and that they should be brought on board as equal partners from the initial stage, and have the same privileges and funding made accessible to them. However, the MNSJ and representatives from the CSJP felt that JSIF was doing an impressive job in meeting and involving their agencies in the process. In addition, negative perceptions of JSIF also included the rigorous approach and expectations of the JSIF team for persons who were a part of the GOALA project and the lack of commitment from community members in beneficiary communities. Some respondents felt that the heavy involvement of the implementing agency, JSIF, had contributed to a confusion in the branding of projects and had difficult speaking to the development agencies that project was associated with.

Capacity development was another theme identified in the implementation of the project. It was felt that a number of the higher-ranking consultancy positions were filled from overseas, which had a negative impact on the development of individual and institutional capacity and the overall sustainability of the project:

> I just want to make a statement based on a lesson learned which is with regards to finding a way to consolidate the approval processes for the project, because, if an implementation agency like the Jamaica Social Investment Fund is given the responsibility to manage the fund and the institution itself has its own approval processes that [it has] a responsibility to carry out in terms of accountability and transparency with the government and the Office of the Prime Minister, I think a significant effort needs to be put into finding a way for the two processes to be consolidated so that there is possibly one, you know, synchronized approval process, you know, not having different approvals going on at the same time or different instances for the same project. (Elite interview, 15 April 2014)

This has resulted in local institutions and people within them missing opportunities for capacity development, and in the public sector experiencing fragmentation. At the governmental level, concerns were also raised because it was perceived that the JSIF, based on the expectations, undermined established structures and chains of command, in the same way that the EU procurement guidelines would supersede GOJ procurement guidelines. Conversely, some identified structural and bureaucratic weaknesses that can exist at the governmental level. When government commitment is absent, weak or variable, project implementation suffers, which impacts on JSIF because of the restrictions within which it must operate.

It was also noted that the rigid nature of the EU guidelines and the challenges understanding the language of the text has impacted on JSIF's ability to effectively and efficiently administer the project objectives. A significant amount of time is invested in ensuring that the manual is strictly followed because the fear of being sanctioned is a constant concern. Much effort is spent to ensure that donor harmonization, alignment and use of country systems are observed during project implementation. However, greater efficiency is achieved with the designation of staff members who are assigned full-time responsibilities to address the various areas and issues that may arise. JSIF also noted other challenges to implementation of PRP II including insufficient capacity of local suppliers and contractors; unnecessary bureaucracy in project administration; inappropriate materials and machinery; mistakes in the installation and start-up of equipment; late arrival of machinery; and unsuitability of imported equipment for local conditions. With the use of creative measures in line with the guidelines, JSIF was able to resolve some of these issues but felt that these would nevertheless have an adverse effect on the sustainability of these projects.

The elite interviews also revealed the desirability of strategic selection of fewer projects or programmes, in order to facilitate more resources being pumped into these communities. This view was strongly supported by participants since it was perceived that it was better to get a small slice of the pie feeding more, than a large slice of said pie feeding fewer. This was perhaps to encourage an increase in the number regranting and an increase in the amount awarded, based on the present harsh limits regarding the maximum acceptable sums that can be sub-granted for any community as stipulated by the European Union. One condition was that the guideline would increase the accessibility for the delivery of sub-grants, because regranting could act as an effective and efficient approach to involve stakeholders and build their capacities. Regranting could also assist in addressing issues precluding many small organizations from applying to calls, given their incapacity to draft accepted proposals (EC 2010).

Monitoring and evaluation and the ability to encourage project sustainability is an important area that needs to be discussed in order to encourage use of best practices and incentivize high performance during implementation. Participants viewed the concept of follow-up of grants as a key performance incentive and an avenue that could reinforce sustainability. For example, it should be mandatory that a five-year maintenance plan be designed in respect of all infrastructure created during these projects, and that people be held accountable for ensuring that the plan is adhered to and periodic checks are made to guarantee sustainability. However, given the duration of a project and the need to minimize funding gaps between the initial and follow-up grants, it may be difficult to reliably assess the performance and outcomes of a given project after only a short period of implementation. The cost-effectiveness and viability of a suitable assessment approach would need to be assessed before the inclusion of this kind of approach, notwithstanding its clear theoretical merits. Indeed, an increased focus on longer-term projects and programmes might reduce the need for follow-up grants to reinforce sustainability (EC 2010).

PRP II: Modules, Guidelines and Procedures Explored

As explained in chapter 1, the EU PCM system is a series of guidelines for each stage of a project's design, implementation and evaluation, which have been applied to projects in various places in Africa, Asia, the Caribbean and the Pacific. It is a complex process in theory and in practice, with manuals specific to each element of the process, and requires extraordinary team work and involvement from all stakeholders to effectively execute a project. As an understanding of the space, culture, politics and the environment is necessary to facilitate effective decision making, the guidelines should also be used in combination with other key reference documents and the pertinent expertise in the relevant areas (EC 2004b). While the projects are primarily targeted toward specific stakeholders, involvement from a wide range of people is also critical in achieving the development goals. Stakeholders such as non-governmental organizations (NGOs), non-state bodies, countries' project managers and community leaders should also be included in discussions centred round design and deliverables of each module. For beneficiary countries, the manuals are interpreted in diverse ways, depending on the experience and work responsibilities of the user, which sometimes results in ambiguity (EC 2004b).

The guidelines encompass the practical guide, financial agreements, technical and administrative provisions, programme estimates and grant contracts.

The Practical Guide

The practical guide is the primary instrument that details contracting procedures that are applied to all EU projects financed from the EU general budget and the European Development Fund (EDF). This is used in the financing and executing of external activities, mainly aid development through geographic and thematic instruments. However, its main focus is guidelines on nationality and rules of origin for public procurement, and grant award procedures (EC 2014).

With the implementation of the amendment to the Cotonou Agreement in 2008, procurement contracts and grants financed under the 10th European Development Fund (EDF 10) have been granted and implemented in accordance with EU rules and procedures and standard documents drafted and published by the European Commission for implementation. The practical guide provides users with the complete information needed for procurement of grants, from the initial procedures to the award, signature and implementation of contracts. The annexes to the document cover both the award and the implementation of contracts, and outlines the contracting measures needed in the direct and indirect organization with ex ante approval or ex post controls by the European Commission (EC 2014).

Under the practical guide, procurement and grant approvals are done under strict instructions to ensure that qualified contractors and grant beneficiaries are chosen without prejudice, and that the best value for money and best prices are obtained, while maintaining transparency and ensuring accountability (EC 2014). The procedures drafted by the European Commission for procurement and award of grants under the appropriate EU external aid programmes are all consolidated in this guide. Any variation requires authorization from the European Commission services in accordance with internal rules (EC 2014). These standards and expectations were all met in the implementation of the PRP II. The tendering and all approval of grant procedures were approved under the financial agreement.

Financial Agreement

This critical country-level document provides the specific requirements and expectations of grant beneficiaries, implementers and EU country representatives (EC 2004a). It is the contract that binds all primary stakeholders and outlines expectations from the community. It was an expectation under PRP II that the country finance a maximum of €10 million while the EDF provided a total of €8.5 million in order to encourage inclusiveness and participation (EC 2014). The EDF 10 funds only 85 per cent of the project and it is the duty of the beneficiary country to provide 15 per cent in order to be awarded the grant funding. This is then transferred at the community level where grants are to be awarded. It is important that evidence is submitted of the community's contribution. This is not limited to cash but can also include services to which the appropriate value is ascribed (EC 2004a).

The agreement also established the parameters of the budget expenditure, addressing issues of cost overruns, handling issues of currencies, places of payment, direct labour operations and procedures for procurement of goods and services. The financial agreement further spoke to the technical and administrative provisions for the execution of the PRP II, and its duration for approximately twenty-four months – December 2011 to December 2013 (EC 2004a).

Technical and Administrative Provisions

The technical and administrative provisions provided a detailed summary of justifications for the implementation of the PRP II, its overall objectives, project purpose, results, activities, indicators, project analysis, lessons learned from past experiences, linkages with other operations, results of economic and cross sectorial appraisals, project implementation, organizational and implementation procedures and monitoring, evaluation and audits. The intended objective of the PRP II, as mentioned in chapter 1, was to foster advancement in the socio-economic conditions and standard of living in select communities. The deliverables were (1) a decrease in the level and frequency of poverty in communities across Jamaica; (2) enhanced capacity of poor communities to contribute to their own development; (3) enhanced access to basic infrastructure and services; (4) enhanced capacity of NGOs to sustain and assist communities and community-based organizations (CBOs) as well as to successfully advance the capacity to liaise with JSIF, SDC, local governments and other organizations relevant to community development; and (5), enhanced capacity of the SDC to assist and support communities (EC 2004a).

Additionally, PRP II used procedures and templates tried and tested during PRP I, which included all relevant documentation, such as the operations manual, field screening handbook, guidelines for project appraisal, community facilities maintenance handbook, project preparation guidelines for day-to-day operations and template of financing agreement with CBOs. Also, all coordination of sub-projects was through the JSIF technical and administrative structure under the supervision of the steering committee. The sub-projects component was demand driven and output oriented. The project management unit and SDC made project recommendations using the criteria and procedures established, from which the steering committee chose approximately forty sub-projects that were then signed off using the financing agreement (PRP model) with each community receiving funding of up to 76 per cent of each project. The local communities contributed at least 25 per cent of the cost of each sub-project in kind by provision of services, or in cash, or as equipment or land. The programme estimate covered the activities implemented and presented elaborated targets and budgets as well as the key indicators by which all achievements were measured. The programme estimate indicated areas of responsibility for the various aspects of the programme components and these were broken down into quarterly activities.

Programme Estimate

The programme estimate is the practical guide that presents instructions for the management of direct labour operations. This was important in the start-up as the programme estimate took six months to be drafted. This was followed by the operational programme that estimated the performance of contracts during the implementation of the programme estimates (EC 2014). The programme estimate is dedicated, authenticated and paid in agreement with the work programme, budget estimate, and the technical and administrative implementing agreements for the relevant programmes, the EDF procedures for awarding contracts and grants, and the instructions of the practical guide in the administration of direct labour operations and programme estimate financed by the EDF (EC 2013).

All contracts and programme estimates had to respect the guidelines and standard documents presented by the commission. All contracts implemented by the financing agreement were awarded and executed in accordance with the overall guidelines for works, supply and services. Contracts were accepted by the African, Caribbean and Pacific countries European Commission (ACP-EC) Council of Ministers, accompanied by the General Conditions for contracts financed by the EDF and the procedures and standard documents presented by the commission for the implementation of external operations (EC 2013).

Grant Contracts

The overall objective for the awarding of grants was to encourage poverty allevi-ation through sustainable growth with a focus on the advancement of commu-nity safety and the decrease of criminal behaviour insusceptible communities. The following results were said to have been achieved: (1) decrease in the level and occurrence of poverty in communities across Jamaica; (2) enhanced capacity of poor communities to engage in their own development; (3) improved access to basic infrastructure and services; (4) enhanced capacity of NGOs to sustain and enable communities and CBOs as well as to successfully develop the capacity to liaise with JSIF, SDC, local government and other organiza-tions applicable to community development; (5) enhanced capacity of the SDC to assist and support communities; (6) prevention and decrease in crime and violence through involvement in volatile communities; and (7) improved access to the justice system through the construction of a courthouse built according to international standards, and incorporating human rights principles and making provisions for children's safety (EC 2014).

These results were based on the primary goals established for the implementation of these projects, but not all goals were achieved. This is despite care taken in the observation stages presented in the grant contract – sub-projects in the overarching financing agreement – and following the prescribed guidelines in the hope of achieving success (EC 2014).

The use of manuals, guidelines and modules are critical to the process because they assist in organizing countries to achieve the ideal principles of development. They also assist in supporting countries in applying these tools in their day-to-day operations. The manuals also aim to enhance the capacity for project implementation in designing projects that are suited to the demands of identified groups; inclusive in relation to the whole project cycle; and acceptable for donors' requirements (Forrester and Sunar 2011). The manual is intended to meet the requirements of donors, implementers and beneficiaries. Its universal project design principles and tools are important for other types of organizations and their partners. Since the target audience is diverse and varied and includes a broad range of organizations, sectors and countries, users will have varied levels of analysis about "aid and development", and also different degrees of language proficiency (Forrester and Sunar 2011). However, with these benefits there are several challenges, and therefore it is important that the manual is introduced with training on how to develop a project proposal, and with the provision of additional reliable support.

For any European Union project to be established, there need to be procedures, guidelines or modules that must be observed as stipulated by the European Union to encourage its successful implementation (Forrester and Sunar 2011). Such successful implementation can only be achieved when the approach to governance is consistent and transparent. Even while all requirements are observed, the results and performance of these projects can be disappointing. Several factors may influence this, including barriers within our existing environment that may result in limits being placed on the potential of implementing agencies to create and expand these projects (Forrester and Sunar 2011). Poor performance can also be as a result of weaknesses in the management of these projects, such as a lack of confidence and leverage in discovering opportunities and developing new ideas and approaches as extrapolated from the data (Forreter and Sunar 2011). Therefore, it is imperative that an examination of these modules be done to encourage optimal performance, the approach of strategic planning processes and incorporation of the procurement of precise skills among project leaders, project staff and community members. It is important to utilize these stakeholders to assist in detecting opportunities. While this capability is clearly valuable when it comes to attaining financial success, the same energy is needed to ensure that the quality of life of beneficiaries of these projects is improved. This in turn involves all stakeholders in the design of these manuals, guidelines and modules while integrating common values, and thinking ahead of intended results. These modifications can encourage sound projects and provide a competitive advantage over other donor agencies in their ability to develop solid and impactful projects.

Despite these challenges, the guidelines presented by the European Union have tried to provide this support and made continuous advancement in the quality of European Commission development assistance. According to the European Commission, "Quality is defined primarily in terms of the relevance, feasibility and effectiveness of the programmes and projects supported by European funds; this also includes how well they are managed" (EC 2004a, 4). The primary mandate of the guidelines is to maintain good management procedures and effective decision making throughout the project management cycle from programming, through to identification, formulation, implementation and evaluation (EC 2004b). The guidelines also try to promote consistency and clarity of approach, while allowing for the operational flexibility required from external assistance programmes. However, this is not always translated into intended outcomes.

Main Discourses Emerging from the Use of the Guidelines

From the analysis, several themes emerged that helped to form the discourse around the guidelines. These themes speak to how the guidelines are interpreted and used, and how they have contributed to the outcomes of the project. The main themes identified and discussed were their rigid and robust nature; culture; frustration with their cumbersome and mechanistic nature, which made them difficult to use; and the limitations placed on implementers in the administration of the projects.

The EU guidelines' templates are said to be "rigid, robust, cumbersome, mechanistic, frustrating to use, and [they limit] your freedom to administer projects" (In-depth interviews 4). Template-based guidelines have always been promoted by the European Union as an acceptable way to initiate, develop and administer projects. Several of their experts claim that templates and their underlying structured language have paved the way toward standardized project management documentation and promoting systems (EC 2014). However, there are some difficulties to this claim. The reality is that the ability to deliver impactful life-changing projects is sometimes lost as project implementers become slaves to the process, and time is wasted trying to understand what is expected. Reference was made in the interviews to the Lucea family courthouse; to revenues being lost; and to a reduction in freedom of expression. With the use of templates, the implementer's personal style and effectiveness are lost. In short, templates are not always beneficial (Gavas, Memon and Britton 2012).

Some reliance on standards, modules and guidelines is needed for successful project implementation. However, it is important to predetermine and detail these procedures in order to produce the desired output and outcome. Modules and guidelines are geared toward cultivating human rights practices or fighting poverty. The outputs or the means to attain these goals are well established. Experience and best practices from other circumstances may be suitable and will need to be relearned as a medium of attempting to address these problems in the hope of achieving development, as these needs and goals change over time and implementers learn from experiences gained during implementation (Koser 2010). If the best approach to addressing challenges is not understood, and if alternate routes are available or inventive solutions are not developed, it can be problematic to address deliverables. What is possible is to have a broad understanding of applicable roles and responsibilities, an embryonic list of tasks and activities and a developing understanding of how to attain outcomes providing room for flexibility during the implementation stage, thus lessening the need to be a slave to the process by placing more emphasis on the project goals (Hummelbrunner and Jones 2013).

While the EU project management tools are traditionally intended to function best in controlled environments, interventions essentially progress without total control and influence over significant factors that will affect their success. The guidelines rely on attaining political and bureaucratic buy-in at numerous stages, but safeguarding ownership can only be prejudiced, rather than guaranteed. For example, interventions that require a combination of resources as stipulated by the European Union, and the collaboration of various actors, are needed in the development of these guidelines.

The European Union established detailed goals and objectives that are shared with persons who are executing the project or who are necessary to its success. After identifying targets, the European Union thoroughly tracks performance against those targets and holds implementers to their achievement (EC 2014). Nonetheless, many of the multidimensional challenges faced in development are as a result of different forms of information and understanding of the evidence, which lead to varied viewpoints between stakeholders on a problem and its causes (Hummelbrunner and Jones 2013). Obstacles to the development of a cooperative understanding of success or measures of growth can occur when several perceptions overlap or conflict. International development involvement often includes a variety of activities executed by a network of partners who have or control the relevant skills and resources. When interventions disregard the agency at any level, they are often ineffective. Success in endorsing policy change is a practical illustration of the need to collaborate, relying on forming coalitions and interacting with broad networks of actors (Hummelbrunner and Jones 2013).

The Complex Nature of the Guide: A Hindrance to Project Success

According to Ramalingam et al. (2008) a complex module increases the reputation of effective management but postures challenges for the tools and methodologies utilized most widely in international development. There are several ways to define "complexity" in economic, social and political development. Based on the nature of the study and the discourse around the text being used, the problem-focused definition is used in grouping the features of complexity according to the kind of issues they present in the design and execution of development interventions: "It is very tedious that you have to go through to read, reread, interpret, cross reference. [It] is really, if you ask me, not necessary. If we could find something very simple that you don't spend a lot of your time going through guidelines, procedure whatever; if we could get a very simple simplified format that would make life a lot easier" (respondent C, 10 April 2014).

The discourse around complexity encompasses three types of challenges: (1) the level of doubt involved; (2) the degree of agreement about project goals or techniques to achieve them; and (3) the degree to which knowledge and capacities are disseminated (Hummelbrunner and Jones 2013). Based on the discourse around complexity, circumstances will hardly ever be compounded in total, with all three types of challenge being clearly present. There is need to focus on the combination and particular significance of the three challenges, which have equal status and can be addressed.

The mix of modalities of operations that the guide represents poses a number of challenges as seen throughout the study. The different modalities themselves are known to be inflexible and this hampered their effectiveness. The EU framework requires that grants are provided based on a call for proposals. However, this is not always seen as the most impartial and transparent mechanism for delivering aid. The "calls" mechanism has been connected to a number of inadequacies by stakeholders, extending from the complexity of the application process and the inability to effectively engage and build the abilities of small local organizations, to the communities with inadequate resources or proposal-drafting knowledge (EC 2014): "Quite frankly those communities will require a lot of hand holding and thinking, I would not say strengthening but I would say more familiarity with what is required" (elite interview 1, 27 January 2014).

There is a general view that there is a need for simplifying the application process for calls. It should be noted that simplification may result in an even more oversubscribed system requiring a lot of hand-holding. It was felt by both SDC and JSIF that this approach was tedious and time-consuming. Therefore, in order for this approach to be considered effective, it means that the requirements of application and grant forms need to be further simplified since there are genuine concerns with regard to literacy, and the ability of community members to understand what is necessary in order to qualify. As one respondent from the elite interview posited: "Sometimes, especially for these small groups, it seemed excessive for them to do all of what we are asking them to do in terms of paper work" (elite interview 5, 6 March 2014).

Another discourse was the applicability of these guidelines to our cultural context and how this has aided in the development process.

Currently, the European Union uses a more asset-based community development (ABCD) approach to development, which requires the community members to be active in the process through co-financing, contributing 20 per cent to the project. This expectation lends itself to some level of flexibility because the participants can contribute cash, use of a building or any other resources accessible to them (grant contract, external action of the European Community, December 2007–December 2011). This is generally supported on the premise as a means to promoting ownership among beneficiaries. However, community members face significant challenges in trying to mobilize the funds required for this contribution. In some cases, this inability to mobilize the required 20 per cent prevents them from applying for funding in the first place, or diverts resources away from their core mandate, which is a key requirement that is stipulated by the guidelines.

Kretzmann and McKnight (1993) posited that ABCD is an approach to community building that accepts that social and economic revitalization begins with what is present within a community, such as, the use of residents within the PRP communities as human resources that are used in the implementation of the projects. This approach involves identifying and mapping available assets in the community by mobilizing them in ways that will assist with multiplying their power and effectiveness. An ABCD approach observes local residents and other community stakeholders as active change agents rather than passive beneficiaries (Garriado, Sey and Hart 2012). This tenet is also a fundamental principle of the bottom-up approach. The ABCD approach builds on assets such as infrastructures that are in the community and mobilizes individuals, associations and institutions to build on their assets and not focus on their needs (Emmerij 2010). This approach firmly believes that the key is to begin to use what is already in the community. Instead of looking through a needs or assets lens to profile the community, look for strengths that can be employed for progress. This will therefore strengthen the community and encourage sustainable projects. The "needs-assessment" approach focuses on the gap between what the community wants and what is missing (Garriado, Sey and Hart 2012). The argument is presented for those working in community development to adopt a more positive approach (Burke et al. 2009). This leads indigenous people thinking in terms of local needs and seeing themselves as "deficient and incapable of taking charge" (Burke et al. 2009, 6). This is in conflict with the primary goal of community development, which is to encourage "positive change in society" by "involving people, most particularly the underprivileged, in making changes and using and developing their own skills" (Burke et al. 2009, 6).

In comparison to the needs-based approach that addresses perceived "deficiencies" through the use of outside experts and resources, the primary mandate of the ABCD approach is to empower citizens and strengthen government and agency. For example, JSIF's effectiveness comes from drawing on local residents' resources, capabilities and knowledge to solve their own problems. At the centre of the ABCD approach is an unfathomable appreciation of the organic steps that citizens take when they instinctively understand the social capital discourse that is influenced by people and relationships, "because people may think that for example they personally benefited from funds that were granted for the projects, that was not so in reality but people perceive it to be so. So sometimes that can exacerbate the difficult social capital situation in the community" (elite interview, respondent 6, April 2014).

Social capital in this context refers to structures of social organization such as linkages, standards and trust that enhance a society's productive potential. It is constructed on the connections that exist within any community that permits persons to excel or advance. Social capital focuses on social relationships, formal and informal relations, and systems, and are treated as assets to mobilize other assets of the community. By considering relationships as assets, ABCD is a practical application of the concept of social capital (Kretzmann and McKnight 1993). Putnam (2007) argued that those who reside in communities with robust social capital have a better sense of obligation to their neighbours and their neighbourhoods; are more comfortable with their existence; and are more likely to find justifiable solutions to local problems from within the community rather than repeatedly and exclusively seeking outside help (Putnam 2000). Kretzmann and McKnight (1993, 7) argued that civil society is debilitated when we remobilize our social service institutions by replacing neighbourly connections with agencies and services.

Critics of ABCD maintain that it is a right-wing approach to community development, which suggests that an underprivileged community has only itself to blame, thus permitting the State to be pardoned of all responsibility (Stoecker 2012). Others posit that the approach undervalues the significance of political and economic systems that impact communities externally (Levinson and Christensen 2003). ABCD is presented by its champions as an alternate to the needs approach, where community leaders are required to concentrate on the needs of their communities to secure funding from external agencies, thus demoralizing the community and making them feel powerless (Levinson and Christensen 2003). However, Stoecker (2012) claimed that the dispute between the needs and assets approaches has been misused. He contends that the risk of disempowering communities follows with the social service method to community change, not the community organizing method that is intended to bring people together to encourage public decisions. However, from the focus group discussion, this was often not the case because a number of community members felt excluded from the process and community leaders felt overworked and disempowered because it was said "it is the same faces you see at each meeting and you have to hunt down other community members to get them to attend community meetings and wait for over an hour before the meeting can start" (respondent elite interview from Focus Group 2, 6 April 2014). However, a general sentiment of creating and fostering dependency was also expressed from the elite interviews by one of the respondents representing the SDC because he expressed a concern for facilitating overdependency. This sentiment was further reinforced in the interview with the representative from the European Union who felt that some of these models were an attempt to encourage overdependency. He noted that projects had start and end dates, which is symbolic of the fact that aid was temporary. If aid was to be beneficial, community members must be involved in the process to encourage sustainability (Stoecker 2012). Cunningham and Mathie (2002) also argued that even an external agency trying to endorse ABCD was in danger of constructing dependency within a community. Therefore, external agencies such as the SDC and CSJP are critical to facilitate the ABCD process but should also know when to step back (Cunningham and Mathie 2002).

The result-based approach is therefore recommended because it provides full financing based on its premise that accessing these services is more a right than a benefit. Access to proper roads, for example, is seen as a right and therefore it is the responsibility of the state to provide access. However, the co-financing requirement may present an actual challenge to the achievement of aid objectives (PIOJ 2012).

The Complexity of the Discourse Issues with Regard to Procurement and Penalties Assigned

In developing countries, procurement guidelines present several challenges because each country has its own economic, social, cultural and political environment that can impact the procurement processes. Disregarding these factors will influence the chances of having a sound procurement system that is intended to achieve proper management and sound policy. The procurement management requirements generally comprise quality, timeliness, financial and technical risks, maximizing competition and sustaining integrity. The procurement policy requirements typically incorporate economic goals, social goals and international trade agreements. It is problematic for policymakers and public procurement practitioners to make an ideal decision, because there are always trade-offs among these goals (Federal Acquisition Institute 1999; Thai 2001). "Procurement for example is a tedious and lengthy process and very confusing process I don't know if it's an issue of the EU modality, of how JSIF does its procurement, or it just has to do with modalities" (respondent 8, April 2014). The aforementioned challenges also include rapid changes in social, political and cultural environments, which have led to new procurement methods being developed. Procurement guidelines cannot be perceived as merely "clerical routines", and they are critical to the effective and efficient implementation of EU projects. However, local practitioners of the procurement process need to be engaged in the design of the guidelines used in the administration of these projects in order to include cultural and environmental nuances that are often unique to the local and political context (Thai 2001).

According to a survey conducted with the 704 members of the National Institute of Governmental Purchasing, Inc., 83 per cent of respondents noted that the major role of current purchasing is tactical (Thai 2001). This therefore suggests that the European Union encourages the use of procurement guidelines to promote greater efficiency by developing research tools that evaluate contemporary trends, strategies, tactics and techniques. These assumptions evolved from the use of these procurement guidelines during project design, implementation and provision of technical support for persons who engaged these procurement guidelines while providing little or no room for flexibility. For the EU procurement guidelines to be properly employed, it is critical that training programmes are developed that are aligned to facilitate exchange of best practices and continuous assessment. This will address some of the arguments presented that questioned their effectiveness and efficiency in the implementation of social development projects.

Procurement is a central function for numerous reasons. First, procurement guidelines have a great impact on the economy and need to be properly managed (Callender and Mathews 2000). Efficiently handling procurement has always been a policy and management challenge for public procurement practitioners as expressed by both PIOJ and JSIF representatives who were interviewed. Second, public procurement has been utilized as a key tool for achieving economic and social objectives (Thai 2001; Arrowsmith and Trybus 2003). This is also critical because the impact of a breach in the administration of the EU guidelines can negatively affect the country becoming a grant beneficiary, or requiring it to repay large sums if a breach is discovered. During the implementation process, breached guidelines will also result in the project being written off as a failure.

The European Union has four objectives for public procurement for projects funded by its grants: (1) making sure that the grant is used to buy only those goods and services needed for the project; (2) ensuring fair competition for all qualified bidders; (3) encouraging transparency or integrity; and (4) promoting development of indigenous contractors and manufacturers by allowing local buyers to build in a margin of preference for those contractors and manufacturers (EC 2004b).

However, these objectives are not always translated into practice and the question is often raised about whom these objectives truly benefit and to what end. A stipulated requirement is that communities contribute a percentage to the funding of these projects. However, their own national procurement guidelines are ignored and the guidelines of the donor agency is viewed as law. This also presents its own sets of challenges with regard to efficiency and effectiveness of some of the goods procured. For example, one instance presented was the purchasing of some equipment during the implementation of PRP II that had voltages that were not compatible with our voltage systems despite following the stipulated guidelines.

Jamaica is currently in the process of adopting a global approach, introduced as a medium to mitigate the challenge of assaying how to fulfil government's procurement regulations and social and economic procurement objectives without violating regional and/or international trade agreements. This issue arises, for example, when complying with national economic policies in the administering of local projects without conflicting with the EU procurement guidelines; and when conflict arises between the two, which regulation supersedes the other and at what stage legally. Also, as markets become more globalized, public procurement practitioners face a greater challenge.

As mentioned earlier, compliance with their governments' procurement laws and policies and international trade requirements force beneficiary countries to face additional encounters such as communication, currency exchange rates and payment, customs regulations, lead-time, foreign government regulations, trade agreements and transportation. However, several external factors contribute to the procurement discourse that also need to be discussed with regard to the EU procurement guidelines and what it represents. These include environmental factors such as market environment, political environment, organizational environment, and socio-economic and other environmental factors.

The market regulates whether or not socio-economic goals of procurement are achieved; whether or not a governmental entity can achieve its needs; the timeliness of achievement; and the quality and costs of purchased goods, services and capital assets. Even under perfectly competitive conditions, some supplies and services are mandated only by the European Union, and are not available in the market or are limited in scope and competition. Apart from procurement regulations and rules issued with regard to the broad legal framework that oversees all business activities inclusive of contract requirements, disputes and breaches are administrated under the same contract law. In developing countries, where legal systems are not inclusive, government contracts may need meticulous provisions because it is sometimes difficult to ascertain which countries' guidelines supersede which, legally.

Different countries have different interests, objectives and beliefs with regard to the use and need for procurement guidelines based on their culture. However, these varied interests help influence the implementation of projects, budget approval and appropriations processes (Thai 2001). Normally, a government programme that is ultimately accepted is a compromise among different views of interest groups, founders, policymakers and management. Implementing agencies must combine various political pressures with sound economic decisions. Should they be concerned with maintaining future relationships at all costs? And what is the best approach to keep funders happy while ensuring that the countries' procurement guidelines are not compromised?

Rigid and Robust Guidelines for Ensuring Good Governance Structures

The European Union prides itself on the guidelines' efficiency, effectiveness, transparency and accountability – all tenets of good governance – and because of their rigidity and robust nature, they are critical in the fight against corruption, especially at the local level. However, in order to suppress the conditions that stimulate corruption, the process needs to be inclusive, meaning it must equally involve the beneficiaries and implementers of these projects. From the interview with the EU representative, it was noted that the European Union accepts the quality of governance structures as part of the discourse in the management of these projects, which is important in encouraging development performance and aid effectiveness. Despite this, it was observed that the influence of these interventions has remained limited. But the question that needs to be asked is: What is the best way to orient overall aid allocations to better reflect governance considerations without having implementers feeling like slaves to a process that is as a result of the rigidity that exists? And has this rigidity contributed to greater project success? The major reports from the evaluation of PRP II have provided few answers on how to address this problem because the challenge presented also raises the question of how we clearly demonstrate these various linkages between rigidity, robustness and good governance models.

Many donors like the European Union already consider governance issues as part of the discourse in the selection criteria for consideration when choosing focus countries or the sum for aid allocations. The World Bank uses the Country Policy and Institutional Assessment "text", which includes governance assessments to help in the assessing of a country's needs for International Development Alliance funding. The Department for International Development (DFID) and the Dutch (European Union) also use this text for assessing development as part of a model to inform their aid allocation (OECD 2000a). Consequently, as with any standardized text of this nature, the Country Policy and Institutional Assessment has some challenges and is not completely sound, methodologically. This makes it difficult to say that the process employed by donors is a rigorous and transparent method of governance assessment and can link this to aid allocation and country projects. Instead, to encourage greater efficiency and management of these projects, measures need to be put in place to support more autonomous, rigorous and detailed governance assessments, incorporating the views of local stakeholders, not only incorporating their views but also building the local capacity to conduct these detailed assessments. As already discussed, these detailed assessments are usually carried out by overseas consultants from donor countries. It is also imperative that we position the level and type of aid according to the exact conditions in each country (OECD 2000b).

Another concern raised is the prolonged time that it takes for governance restrictions to be overcome because the sub-discourses are also seen as political and localized, with consideration being given to the space in which this operates. However, recent discourses around increasing implementation of successful projects assume that governance structure can be improved quickly to encourage this success. Historically, there was no shortcut to constructing sound institutions in poor countries. Governance is critical to the process and is key in the discourse around development performance and aid effectiveness. More focus needs to be directed to evaluating governance discourse in an inclusive, rigorous and independent manner, pulling on the views of local stakeholders. Better orienting of aid interventions to governance contexts would help make development assistance more effective, which would result in a reduction of aid duplication and would benefit both poor people in developing countries and reassure taxpayers in donor countries (Hydén, Court and Mease 2004).

Culture (One Size Fits All) and the Guidelines

The globalization of project management manuals and guidelines does not mean a globalization of culture. Cultural nuances have impacted the execution of international development projects. Different understandings of other countries' standards may result in difficulties when implementing these international projects. In order to circumvent these cultural challenges, donor countries and agencies need to remember that different actions and practices of other countries' representatives are due to different cultural values. What can be appropriate behaviour in one culture can be interpreted as impolite and insulting in another. This can have serious implications on how stakeholders engage with each other and the quality of work produced by individuals that can hamper efficiency during implementation.

Additionally, language is a critical component to the discourse; this is further explored in chapter 3. In order for communication to be efficient and effective, it first needs to be understood that cultural differences exist and that the discourse of language is usually manifested in three ways: language beyond the level of a sentence; language behaviours linked to social practices; and language as a system of thought (Becker 1991). Each of these is influenced and shaped by cultural meanings and symbolic interaction. It is key that this is remembered when we engage the guidelines at the initial and implementation stages of the project. For example, a word might not mean the same thing universally, and the definition that is often assigned is based on the context and the environment in which it is being used. Therefore, a universal and generalized definition cannot be ascribed to all words since conflict and confusion may arise at the implementation stage when local project managers are tasked with assigning the correct interpretation to the words (Becker 1991).

A one-size approach does not fit all. This means that all local projects cannot be approached in exactly the same way as stipulated by the guide. The project objectives, deliverables, participants, partners or executors are all different with different experiences and expertise that help to shape their discourse and influence their approach. It is also important to remember that the guidelines were first written for Africa, whose reality, environment and needs are different from those in the Caribbean and, within that, Jamaica. This further raises the question of whether a regional approach to project development and implementation is possible. At the regional level, many Caribbean countries share a common history but a different interpretation of that history and culturally strong differences exist. Nicholas and Steyn (2008) argued that there are four concerns in an international project, most of which involve aspects of the project's locality: local institutions and culture, local stakeholders, local natural environment and local technology. The World Bank reports that international projects are being prejudiced by cultural and social differences of the implementing enterprises, technological and infrastructural differences, and religious differences between countries (World Bank 2006).

Culture forms part of the discourse that is established by patterns of thought, feelings and possible actions that each individual may take – not as abstraction, but as a result of continuous learning. Notwithstanding the multiplicity of minds, there is a system that serves as the preliminary point for mutual understanding, composed of dimensions of cultural difference that makes it difficult to manage the expectations of the guide. House et al. (2004) looked at the different dimensions of national cultures and noted that there were similarities and differences identified as (1) power distance, (2) individualism versus collectivism, and (3) uncertainty avoidance. This forms a dimensional model of the differences between national cultures and countries (Hofstede and McCrae 2004). For example, a theme that recurred when participants were asked about cultural differences in Jamaica related to the regard for time, or the "bly" mentality. (A "bly" is a favour or chance.) Universally this is not an accepted approach. However, at the local level, culturally, that is a practice that is recognized, so often tardiness is not greeted with the same amount of sanctioning as in other parts of the world as the offender is "given a bly". It is important that these simple examples be kept in mind because they can have serious implications regarding cost and time of completion, which are both critical to project success.

Rodrigues and Sbragia (2012) discussed the notion of hierarchical distance and its relationship to high performance. This can be applied to the Jamaican context, where informal and formal hierarchical structures exist in a number of communities – for example, the roles of community leaders and "dons" in the day-to-day operations of the community. This approach is, however, not unique because there are several studies that examine the role of the informal structures and the implications for community livelihood. This is a known reality that exists. Therefore, a response or approach must be put in place as a medium to mitigate this, which will encourage further community development. However, the guide does not take into account these challenges and project managers are often forced to be creative to try and address this issue of hierarchy. While this practice of the informal hierarchical distribution of power is not lauded or encouraged, it is important that the guide speaks to measures to mitigate this challenge, which will impact project success and, by extension, community development.

Top-Down versus Bottom-Up Approaches

A common theme throughout the discussion was an expressed frustration with the use of the top-down approach as facilitated by the model in the implementation of the EU PRP II projects. A number of the respondents felt that they were not included in the decision-making process in the identification of the priority areas and what would better represent their needs:

> Before them decide to establish programme them need fi meet with the youth in the community, because it wouldn't be only us here; they would have to meet with the rest of the community, discuss this with them and find out who is interested and who is not and then we could take it back to you now and say "we have out of 30 we have 15 people interested". Because every time them people come with project and nobody no interested in them a who decide them projects here? They no see is education, job and road we need, not no fishing plant. And who must maintain it? (Focus Group 1, 2014)

From the focus group excerpt presented above, a number of reasons were presented against the use of a top-down approach, and the benefits of utilizing the bottom-up approach can be extrapolated. One key factor is that it shows respect for the ideas of people living in the community who are the beneficiaries of these aid programmes. It also recognizes the existence of diverse needs with regard to social and economic cohesion, for balance and sustainable development, and encourages good governance structures such as transparency. Despite the fact that projects are selected using the community profiling approach provided by the SDC, there still remain questions regarding the validity of the methodology used in determining these priority areas. Sanyal (1988, 51) posited:

> Development from below, bottom up development, needs based approach, grassroots development are some of the phrases planners coined twenty-five years ago, to support an alternative development model for poor countries. Implicit in these phrases were assumptions about what was wrong with the dominant development paradigm, popularly called the top down/trickle down approach. . . . The top down model had failed because the institutions created to foster development from the top had themselves become the greatest hindrance to development.

The bottom-up approach for project development can also be credited for building consensus through participatory decision making because it ensures broad and fair involvement from all project stakeholders. Inclusion of the local community by obtaining active contribution of its economic and institutional partners and associations in the development process requires systematizing the dissemination of information, and enabling access to training while guaranteeing transparent decision-making procedures by giving renewed confidence to local communities and players not accustomed to expressing their needs, expectations or plans (Patras and Kenakap 2010). If this is achieved, it will encourage these communities to share thoughts and produce initiatives that require a degree of open-mindedness and acceptance of the risks associated with innovation. Along with this, a culture will also be created that will promote meetings and discourse between people, convergence between sectors, and the exchange of information and skills among a multitude of target groups (Patras and Kenakap 2010).

The bottom-up approach for development projects allows local players and community members to express their views and provides an opportunity to help these individuals with defining their developmental needs. This participatory method is often seen more as a development approach than a day-to-day reality. However, there are concerns raised about the guidelines, and with efforts to put local communities and local development stakeholders back at the heart of the rural development, the bottom-up approach encourages local participation in the development of policy. The involvement of local players is needed at all levels, either through consultation or by involving them in the partnership as stipulated by the guide.

Scholars such as Matland (1995) have put forward several arguments against the bottom-up approach and instead place emphasis on the top-down approach as the most viable option. One argument that has been postulated points to an increase in the level of efficiency because top-down theorists request a clear and consistent statement of the policy goals, a minimization of the number of involved actors and a limitation of the extent of change necessary (Matland 1995). However, the most prominent criticism of this approach is the way it views the single actors within the process (Matland 1995), favouring the decision makers as key actors, which leads to greater project success because it eliminates back and forth with aid beneficiaries to whom not much attention is given. This is seen as a more definitive approach to decision making.

In addition, the European Union acknowledges the fact that implementers at the micro-level think about their work and form their own opinions about the tasks they receive. Through a process of monitoring and evaluation, they identify changes needed for the programme to improve or be better adapted to the circumstances. Bottom-up theorists are criticized, however, for over-evaluation of the degree of actual local independence from the policy-makers, because the implementation could not work without the resources and institutional structure provided by funders. From a financial standpoint, the top-down approach is said to be a more viable option because funders can feel a loss of financial control by following a bottom-up approach. Implementers fear the often-unstructured nature of the communities and the possibility of corruption (Matland 1995). A prime example presented was the number of family members that comprised the community development committee in one community, a body that represents the interests of citizens, is the voice of the community and acts as liaison. This raises the question of representation on community bodies and issues of corruption and accountability when this approach is used to involve community views in a bottom-up approach.

These factors play a key role in a project's success or failure. However, the bottom-up approach permits funders to communicate goals and objectives through a participatory approach while community members are encour-aged to feel involved in the developmental process of these objectives. Doing this further encourages the beneficiaries of the programmes to treat major project milestones as their own, thus fostering a certain level of pride. It also allows the beneficiaries to think more creatively because they feel a part of the project and know that their initiatives are appreciated, thus building morale. The bottom-up approach can also be viewed as a way of managing informa-tion, donor's expectations and how they benefit from aid. The primary goal of the bottom-up approach is the establishment of livelihood approaches of all stakeholders involved in the operation of the project, regardless of cultural and socio-economic differences. Bottom-up approaches have to overcome some challenges, the most prominent being that of building consensus around the measures needed to encourage project success and engage indigenous citizens and community organizations in the decision-making processes. If this is done, it will increase efficiency and increase the project's sustainability as a result of community members' willingness to develop a community sense of owner-ship for the programmes (IFAD 2009). Direct community support and local government attitude to share a common emphasis on participatory, decen-tralized, and multisectorial planning, execution, and governance is needed. Community assistance, such as equivalent funds and co-production activi-ties, encourages recipient ownership and helps guarantee that investments are demand driven. While different methodologies of mobilizing governance and convenience at the indigenous level offer specific strengths, each method is also inadequate by its entry point and approaches. Linking different approaches can, therefore, capitalize on the comparative advantages of each, completing their specific contributions (IFAD 2009).

The Mechanistic Approach and Restarting of Development Aid

The discourse around development is political because there are several players and variables that have contributed to development success. The main driver for development success is foreign aid, defined as the flow of resources (monetary and non-monetary) from the developed countries to the least developed countries (Easterly 2003). Grants are considered to be the most desired type of foreign aid since they represent a net addition to the resources accessible for development purposes. Aid flows into Jamaica have been considerable, but remain fragmented, and focus primarily on the agreements with donor countries for satisfying short-term needs, rather than on a collective, longer-term view on broader economic and governance fundamentals. Sachs et al. (2004) argued that aid is crucial in enabling countries to escape low-growth inducing poverty. Aid flows toward developing countries also lead to a transmission of knowledge and technical assistance, and pave the path for future development (Sachs 2002). It is said that foreign aid helps developing countries in the construction of infrastructure, employment generation, increasing absorptive capacity, and the setting up of heavy industries (Sachs 2002). However, aid also has a negative effect on growth as countries have to service debt and the wishes of the donor countries have to be fulfilled. Further, demands for rapid structural changes are difficult to address, political motives have to be granted, and monetary inflow of aid can also lead to corrupt activities. Aid-recipient countries often develop a dependency syndrome, reduction in savings and social tensions (Shah 2012), all of which lead to aid effectiveness in developing countries being a controversial and debatable topic.

However, it is important that the European Union clearly establishes its contribution and mark regarding the impact and outcomes, which are further explored in chapter 4. Because of this, emphasis is usually placed on hard projects, often said to be "sexier", since one can easily point to a result. For example, a main component of PRP II was crime reduction. In an effort to achieve this, a number of police stations and court houses were rehabilitated. Despite these efforts, during that time there was a spike in crime, raising questions as to whether or not a soft project looking at the resocialization of community members would not have been more beneficial in achieving this goal.

Another issue is the sustainability of these projects, which is further discussed in chapter 5. A number of the projects implemented often lack the infrastructural requirements needed to maintain them. With any project, there is a start and end date, because the question asks: What happens at the end of the project? What usually occurs is a restart. The efforts are terminated until another donor agency considers this a priority area when efforts are once again made to create the same plan to address the said so-called needs of the community.

International agencies and governments of developed countries have also made efforts to mobilize resources so as to increase aid. But critics of aid contend that it has historically been incompetent in effecting development, and growth in aid funds is therefore undesirable (Shah 2012). However, a transitional focus is that an increase in aid can be anticipated under specific conditions that guarantee that aid is likely to succeed in encouraging growth and development, such as when countries have "good policies" in place.

Another reason for this repeated restart is that aid has been reactive and lacks the leverage to inspire or empower institution-building or to create powerful incentives to reform. This phenomenon is not new. Donors are aware of this issue, and have tried to establish multilateral financing mechanisms and new aid coordination bodies, such as the implementation of the Task Force on the PRP II. This was done in an attempt to encourage and give a voice to different stakeholders in the selection of sub-projects or GOALA projects implemented. However, the effectiveness of these structures is questioned with regard to who has the power to determine the effectiveness of the outcomes.

Another problem is the inability of development aid to rapidly resume programmes in post-crisis situations. This is why longer-term project engagements are encouraged by the humanitarian mandate in the area of developmental activities. For example, development cooperation often ignores the hazards of droughts or conflicts and the need to guard susceptible households by helping them to establish coping strategies. How much aid do we need to prevent this continuous restart of development? The discourse around this is very controversial and has been and still continues to be debated by scholars. In addition, different discourses depict different pictures. While many studies found aid to have a positive impact on growth, others found that it hampers growth. Additionally, aid is often misused based on conditions set out in agreements that the beneficiary must use expensive goods and services from donor countries. Much aid does not actually go to the poorest who need it the most but instead aid amounts are gathered by rich country protectionism that contradicts market access for poor country products. Rich nations use aid as a control mechanism to open poor country markets to their products and large projects or massive grand strategies often fail to help the vulnerable because money can often be embezzled away (Green 2012).

Deterministic and Mechanistic Environmental Factors: Reasons for Project Failure

Developing countries like Jamaica are aware of the urgency and need to integrate environmental concerns into project formulation, implementation and appraisals, which are as a result of the mechanistic and deterministic approach that these environmental factors have had in contributing to the success of projects. Natural disasters as well as factors in the political, cultural, technical and economic environment have had both positive and negative impacts on the scope, time and resource allocation in the administration of the EU PRP II.

Countries that have more political stability are likely to showcase better project performance. Srebrnik (2000) is among several authors who observed that a characteristic of small islands is their capability to sustain democratic political systems. Political instability joined with underdeveloped institutions and an absence of knowledge may result in frequent changes of government, or may inspire unexpected modification of policies affecting the successful achievement of development project objectives. The point is that political factors at the national and regional levels must be addressed. In addition, several obstacles are created by inconsistency in policies, laws and regulations and the variations in the use of government and EU guidelines, all of which contribute to inefficiency. A major concern was the GOJ's current governance by its own sets of procurement guidelines, which are sometimes not in sync with those of the European Union. This caused misunderstanding and raised concerns with regard to expectations among implementers, because it was often felt that breaches would occur. A standardization process of all procurement processes and procedures, both at the local and international levels, is currently underway. From a development project's perspective, factors such as the ones already mentioned contribute to an environment of uncertainty, and represent limitations in project outputs and reach.

The localization of knowledge during the development and implementation stages is critical to a projects' success because the goals and objectives must be practical and created with an understanding of the cultural nuances that exist. Staudt (1991, 35) says, "Understanding culture is the starting point for learning the meaning of development management, the values that guide people's actions, and the behaviour of administrators." For the purpose of this discussion, this is the position from which we view the cultural factor in the context of international development projects. Cultural differences appear in many forms of development settings, from assumptions, to project design, to technology transfer and management styles. From the elite interviews, it was noted that the EU PRP II required implementers to engage foreign consultants to assist with project preparation and implementation because of the lack of technical or organizational skills accessible in the recipient countries. The international consultants, however, viewed and executed their roles through different lenses based on different sociocultural backgrounds than the recipients, they were not accustomed to indigenous resources and were not familiar with different approaches to local informal project management practices. This resulted in frustration, conflict of interest and placed extra pressure on local implementers that restrained or obstructed project progress. A cultural misfit relative to project goals and a lack of indigenous knowledge and understanding results in refusal of the project by beneficiaries.

Another environmental factor that must be considered is the digital divide that exists, because the level of technology in developing countries is not necessarily the same as that in the donor country. Therefore, variations will occur in design, manufacturing, procurement, creation, equipment installation, and operation of the equipment and its compatibility with accomplishment of project objectives (Staudt 1991). These differences result in a lack of sufficient resources, technical and managerial skills, and lower human capital productivity. An elite interview confirmed this behaviour as an event regarding the use of voltage in the installation of a particular machine was recounted. Based on the variation that existed, the machine procured was not as efficient and, as such, a purchase was not seen as the most viable option. Although some of these technological differences may be addressed by keen management, this also poses its own challenges as was demonstrated in one situation. Nuances in the management of the project by the EU project sponsor resulted in a slow and cumbersome decision-making process and lack of training of the local staff for sustainability. This point was particularly noted by all persons interviewed, because reference was constantly made to the JSIF PRP II project manager as the only expert capable of dealing with matters and providing explanations with regard to EU procedures and guidelines.

A known requirement for the implementation of the project is that the GOJ and the communities who are the beneficiaries of the programme are expected to contribute either cash or other resources to encourage greater partnership and buy-in. But this is not always feasible, based on local economic conditions and the high levels of poverty. Another contributing factor is that government's priorities and economic agenda or primary objectives might not be considered an area of focus by the European Union during that time frame. Also, acts of God such as floods, earthquakes or hurricanes may affect plans. Corruption, defined by the World Bank as "the abuse of public office for private gain" (World Bank 2011, 2) can also have an adverse effect economically. Inevitable political intrusion along with a lack of transparency and regulatory institutions, bribery and corruption are widespread in international development projects, resulting in ineffective use of development resources. However, with the effective implementation of the procedures and guidelines, the European Union has managed to have minimal issues in this regard, because the guidelines are reputed to be sound in relation to the tenets of good governance structures. Yet these factors are key aspects that the guidelines failed to have built into their modality. This was a common theme throughout the examination of the project management discourse, since the guidelines, as the prescribed text, failed to look at the political, physical and cultural environment, which are all key areas that can contribute to the successful implementation of the project.

The Use of Language in the European Union Representation of the Text

Language was a central component in the implementation of the EU PRP II project both in terms of construction and function; that is, language was used as the primary means for guiding the process and as a means of constructing, rather than mirroring, reality (Eade 2010). Language was also used as a form of social action. The text guides the implementation process to achieve project goals, for example to attribute responsibilities and assign penalties when one fails to follow the guidelines. One respondent from the elite interviews said, "You have to become very familiar with the language because the EU really has its own language for defining the operational framework" (respondent 8, April 2014). This operational framework is a critical component in the discourse. Therefore, the use of language in examining how the guidelines are constructed between the implementers and beneficiaries accounts for the variability and exploration of the rhetoric (Potter 2003). Discourses also entail subject positions, which speakers take up when they employ language, based on their cultural reality, and this has fundamental consequences both for the implementers and beneficiaries of the programme.

Figure 3.2 represents the ecological manifestation of language for the EU PRP II, which was created by the researcher. The diagram shows the different discourses around the text and how the text was manifested and translated at each stage.

Yule (2006, 126) viewed "text" as "the verbal record of a communicative act". Text can be divided into written and spoken forms. Focusing on the written form, "a text may be differently presented in different editions, with different type-face, on different sizes of paper, in one or two columns; variations exist, from one edition to the next". This was a recurring challenge based on the interviews conducted, because persons at different stages of the implementation

Community

The
implementation
agency

Process of
interpretation

EU manual
text

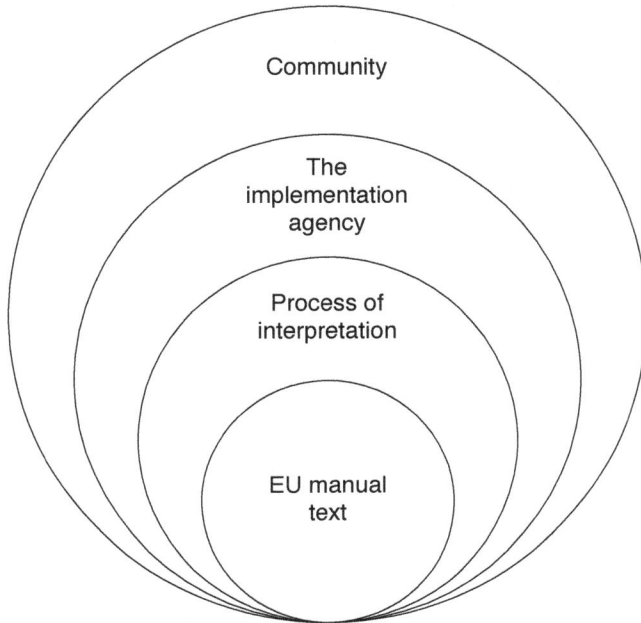

Figure 3.2. The ecological manifestation of language and the EU PRP II
Source: Walters (2012)

process were sometimes confused about which version of the text to use, since the text had several updated versions. This led to the challenge of aspects of the text being edited during the implementation stage and this edit was not always communicated, which often resulted in the implementers applying incorrect procedures and having to take responsibility for whatever sanctions were assigned for such mishaps. A mitigation strategy put in place by a number of the implementers was to constantly check the website and examine the document for any changes that might have occurred. This impacted on time and was considered an unproductive approach to achieving project success.

Language as Construct: The Practical Use of the Guidelines to Achieve Development

Language as a construct looks at all the assumptions created by explicit versions of the phenomena and procedures that the text attempts to describe (Yule 2006). The guidelines are the prescribed text used by implementers during the initiation, implementation and evaluation of the project. The guidelines are used throughout the entire project cycle for the sole purpose of achieving project success, which is the eradication of poverty. The first approach in examining the construct is to scrutinize the various ways in which the objects under study are created in the specific text. All occasions where the object is stated or implied focus on the variability in the constructions after establishing the different modes of the object. This broadens our focus to locate these constructions within culturally available systems of meaning (Widdowson 2007).

For example, I posited that the use of the guidelines and the impact it has had on the implementers and beneficiaries of the programme throughout the duration of this study had positive and negative effects. As discussed throughout, there are still areas that need to be strengthened to encourage greater success and sustained development. The justification and approach of the European Union were also explored because the interview with the EU representative reminded of the need for the guideline or module. Respondent 1 revealed this was needed to encourage greater accountability, efficiency and effectiveness. This objective was achieved, because a common theme throughout was the rigid nature of the module to encourage greater accountability, and its ability to minimize corruption and misappropriation of funds. In addition, its ability to standardize approaches are viewed as both negative and positive. This is a consequence of countries' diversity based on cultural and governmental structures such as in the Caribbean. Although the islands share a common history, they vary in practices and cultural nuances and these need to be considered when the text is being constructed. Also, the text was originally designed for the continent of Africa. Despite the similarities of general principles governing developing countries, variations do exist and these can and will have an impact on the use of the model to achieve project and development success.

Language as Functional: Rhetoric Strategies Used by Stakeholders to Encourage Development

The dynamics of the interaction between the participants' use of language (beneficiaries) and management of the interaction (the implementers and EU country representative) were also examined, taking into consideration the programme estimate, procurement guidelines and the grant application guidelines, and the responsibility and sanctions that applied with the assignment of roles and responsibilities. Language explains how these guidelines are organized and the rhetorical strategies used by the European Union to encourage and promote their version as credible, objective, reliable and rational. In examining the function of the text, which references both written and spoken words, the European Union's dialogue in relation to the discursive context of its pre- and post-production were also considered. This evidence is supported in various evaluation reports done by both external and internal entities. The data from the elite interviews and focus group discussions highlighted several challenges based on how the text was written and issues related to translation, because the use of some words and the context in which they are used are often lost in translation. Also analysed was the function that the deployment of specific discourses had on the unfolding interaction, such as the use of a top-down approach instead of the bottom-up approach, which may be a more viable option for project selection. The levels of involvement by the community were explored, and this is all affected by the use of language. A common concern was the complexity of the forms that persons at the community level were expected to complete and their inability to do so.

The discursive agenda of all stakeholders needs to be considered to acquire true project success, because all stakeholders view the language that is presented through different lenses and set their agendas based on perceptions. For example, even though all parties involved approach the process as a viable option to alleviate poverty and to achieve true development success through aid, there is a disconnect in the methodology used to try to obtain these objectives. Beneficiaries believed that they needed to be more integral and involved while the implementers of the project felt that the procedures were far too rigorous and lacked flexibility. Consequently, they aspired to more autonomy during the implementation stage. The European Union, on the other hand, sees their own approach as having minimal flaws and as the best approach to encourage standardization and accountability. However, the success of this module is often questioned and the response is given based on the perceived lens through which each stakeholder views the representation of their reality, a concept that this researcher refers to as the discursive agenda. This is relevant as the notion that refers to the effects that each participant's talk has on the overall interaction. The agenda of each participant can be deduced only after the detailed analysis of the function of their talk.

The Use of Language as a Medium of Positioning and the Voices Used

Another important notion is that of subject positioning, that is the characteristics made relevant through precise ways of talking (Davies and Harré 1990). This approach is seen in relation to the specifics of the interaction and to wider discourses that were carried out during the evaluation stage and the voices that were represented. The interaction when both implementers and beneficiaries spoke and how they are addressed or are spoken about in the guidelines, and their positioning in the text was examined. A primary area for the researcher based on the information garnered was who had the most active voice. This was identified to be the European Union, which awarded them a position of power. The voices of the beneficiaries and implementers were also examined as active agents for change in the modifications made to manuals and procedures used. However, several persons from both the elite interviews and focus group discussions felt this was not the case and greater effort needed to be put in place to ensure that these voices were translated and manifested in recommendations that could be used for future projects. There is a reciprocal relationship between discourses and practices; dominant discourses, which become taken for granted, support and enable social and institutional practices, which in turn maintain them (Davies and Harré 1990).

The analytical question raised also looked at the roles assigned, especially with regard to considerations of power and resistance, which can take the form of a subtle use of the discourse. This sometimes led to a refusal to access the grants based on the complexity of the process and language. The perceived powerlessness or lack of voice by beneficiaries and programme implementers and issues of subjectivity – which is also seen as their inability to locate themselves in the EU PRP II project – were concerns raised by the SDC. This resulted in the inability of communities to identify various project deliverables and successes with the European Union, despite being clearly visibly branded as such, but instead identified these deliverables with JSIF. This was noted during the focus groups when the question of output was raised. Despite the fact that the building used to facilitate the focus group discussion was clearly marked as a building sponsored by the European Union, the focus group respondents felt that the building was the sole product of JSIF.

The EU Guidelines: A Vehicle for Foreign Aid Dependency

The EU guidelines represent the EU mode of operation. EU aid projects have been accused of being a vehicle promoting and fostering aid dependency and this was echoed by several respondents during the interviews. This led to the debate on whether this vehicle of donor funding and the use of prescribed guidelines are beneficial, responsible for transporting countries like Jamaica to development success, or transporting us to a culture of reliance and dependency. Since the initiation of modern foreign aid, the debate on various aid-related issues has continued. In general categorization, there are literatures and notable scholars supporting and opposing foreign aid. However, several agencies such as the European Union applaud the benefits of foreign aid as a medium of alleviating poverty. This is achieved with the assistance of the guidelines that encourage greater accountability and minimize the level of corruption, ensuring that resources are spent and located in accordance with what they were identified for. However, this discussion forces us to focus on a bigger discussion of whether or not foreign aid is a positive or negative force in development.

The EU Modality Equals Foreign Aid Dependency

The discourse around foreign aid has evolved over the years and has taken on several meanings and representations. Lancaster (2007) attempted to differentiate the discourses, the particular objectives and effective delivery of foreign aid. This added voice was an extension of the critical post-development discussion. In addition, from a post-development standpoint, there are several terminologies that are used to identify foreign aid throughout the literature. Most common are developmental aid, foreign aid, development assistance, emergency aid, bilateral aid and multilateral aid (Lancaster 2007). According to Riddell (2007), foreign aid is defined as all resources – physical goods, skills and technical know-how, financial grants (gifts), or loans – transferred by donors to recipients (Lancaster 2007; Riddell 2007). Finding that this definition was incomplete, this researcher would like to add, "in order to achieve an agreed objective or developmental goal". For example, the primary purpose for PRP II was poverty alleviation and, by extension, a reduction in crime. It was hoped and promised that this aid provided by the European Union would meet these expectations and would bring the country closer to achieving its developmental goals. The question of whether or not this was achieved is one that needs further exploration. The elite interviews highlighted mixed feelings, because people thought that on the surface, the objectives appeared to have been met to some extent, but felt that deeper analysis would show that this was not the case, since the methodology used had flaws that affected the project's success.

However, as each donor country designs its foreign aid policy and establishes the quantity to be allocated to a recipient, variations exist in the details that are based on self-interest. Historical and political factors shape the basis for extending aid. The main motives are (1) to support emergency needs; (2) to support development goals; (3) to show solidarity; (4) self-interest; (5) historical ties; (6) to contribute to the global public good and security; and (7) to promote human rights (Riddell 2007). These motives are consistent with those set out in EDF 10.

The self-interest argument highlights the notion of dependency and its negative connotations. The concept of development has also been accused of falsely representing a country's reality by creating images of using aid to live beyond its means, and so "depending" on aid to support its standard of living. However, the definition of aid dependence may be incorrectly construed based on different interpretations of the term. A country that appears to require large aid inflows to either sustain or achieve modest improvements in living standards is said to be aid-dependent. In addition, a state that relies on donors to provide basic requirements needed for comfortable living and access to these resources can also be considered as fostering and creating a culture of dependence that can be agreed to be negative (Randel and German 1998).

The EU Guidelines Encourage Aid Dependency

A country is considered to be aid-dependent when the government cannot perform many of the core functions, such as delivering basic public services, without relying heavily on aid from donor countries. When countries such as Jamaica rely heavily on aid for a significant portion of their funding, this dependency will have a negative impact on the relationship that exists between citizens and their governments, who are no longer held accountable for delivering services to address social conditions such as poverty eradication. In such situations, governments channel their attention on their associations with aid donors rather than on those with their own people, and citizens focus attention on the provision of services by donors. An example of this was raised in an elite interview when the interviewee reflected that it was important to ensure that aid provided was properly branded: "If a building is worked on it is important that persons identify this as a EU project and not just a JSIF project as community members sometimes get confused with who is responsible for fixing up the police station and are quick to identify this as solely a JSIF initiative" (elite interview 6, April 2014).

While aid is successful in contributing to human development, dependency on foreign aid can be more challenging, because it prevents local economic development or mobilization of domestic resources. It also undercuts countries' capability to decide on their own development approaches, which is what is needed for development to be achieved (Herbert 2006).

The guidelines are also accused of creating aid dependency within the communities that are forced to respond to the ever-changing enthusiasms imposed on them by donors. This may alleviate the worst aspects of poverty but stifle development of the political discipline and managerial habits needed for self-reliance (Green 2012). Aid-dependent governments can lose their autonomy to design and execute their own home-grown development policies and define priority areas as a direct consequence of aid, because they are so busy with donors who may insist, for instance, on recipient countries implementing the donors' requirements. As one respondent from the elite interview noted: "We like to be much more on the side to empower the communities, teach them how so that they can aid in their own development; train them on how to push forward their own projects and liaise with the government, with the NGOs; but here we have done a lot for infrastructure, building classrooms, roads. Of course, the method is always the same" (elite interview 5, March 2014).

Therefore, the real success of aid must be measured based on genuine sustainable development progress, which empowers the citizens to hold their governments accountable and empower governments and community members to develop their own economies and end their dependence on aid (Green 2012).

Summary

Despite the benefits and the best practices garnered from using the guidelines, similar to any other sets of guidelines, the European Union brings its own challenges such as its cumbersomeness and rigid nature.

Arising from the development dialogue and the development discourse were the continuous restarts of the development process and its lack of flexibility. This discussion was framed around the current arguments of development aid and the way donors and beneficiaries engaged its allocation. A key area of justification for the use of the modules and guidelines is their ability to encourage accountability, transparency and to minimize the level of corruption often associated with aid projects.

However, a one-size-fits-all model is not always ideal for project success because factors such as culture, political structure and formal and informal leadership all contribute to the indigenous approach that needs to be employed when implementing projects. The bottom-up approach to development is also suggested as a more practical approach in the implementation of these social projects. The European Union does not operate in a vacuum and like all donor agencies prides itself on its ability to create and foster partnerships.

The communities were also seen as an important element in the discursive structure. An examination of the ability of the European Union and JSIF to involve the communities as active participants while encouraging community growth and development were also explored. The role of language as a function for the rhetoric strategies used by the European Union was an essential component in its positioning and representation of voices. Social and environmental factors were also observed, based on the mechanistic and deterministic impact that they have had on achieving project success and the creativity employed by JSIF as the chief implementing agency was also discussed as key elements contributing to the discourse.

The chapter also examined Foucault's definition of power, which is an important characteristic in defining the discourse that exists when trying to craft an analysis of the implication of the existence of partnership in the conceptualization and implementation of the project. The European Union is presented throughout this chapter as the main driver of power. This results in a discussion surrounding the impact of power on identified needs, resulting in what I have termed as the continued restart to development. I further explored the impact of the structural nature that is required for communities to ensure that they qualify for this aid that is said to further enhance their development. Issues of accountability and transparency are also explored as I looked at some of the best practices associated with using the module despite varied cultural nuances that may exist that have hindered greater success of PRP II. With regard to the discourse and associated structures, an examination of the stakeholder is critical to the discussion in understanding the discourse that exists.

4.

The Myth of Development
Project Outcome and Impact

The contradiction of the relationship between developing countries' community movements and international development institutions is that both subscribe to the same objectives and both require what the other has, yet they have had several challenges in their attempts at working together. The expectations of both parties in the relationship continue to be managed and re-evaluated in an attempt to achieve development. The European Union, at times, views community organizations as unstable amateur partners in the serious business of development (elite interview, April 2014) and communities sometimes view development agencies such as the European Union as the saviour in all social ills and the cure for all that is wrong developmentally (focus group discussion, April 2014).

An expectation that is often misconstrued is that aid will foster development. This is not the case; poverty has increased to one-fifth of the Jamaican population (PIOJ/STATIN 2012). Remarkably, poverty increased in most urban areas but fell in a number of rural areas owing primarily to increased earnings from agriculture. Poverty prevalence increased by 2.3 percentage points relative to 2010 to reach 19.9 per cent (PIOJ/STATIN 2012). This was further supported in the elite interview discussions where it was noted that there was a spike in crime during the PRP stipulated time period. "As a matter of fact the very period of PRP II could have been the highest level of murders in the community over the period" (elite interview, April 2014). Despite the provision of aid through the administration of the PRP II, there was in fact an increase in poverty and crime in some of the targeted communities, based on reports from the Ministry of Justice and the PIOJ.

Figure 4.1 showcases the impact framework diagram that explores the impact of social development projects and the need for impact, output, effective leadership, sustainability, good governance structures, monitoring and evaluation techniques, and capacity building. It also demonstrates the interconnectedness of the roles and the impact each has on preventing aid dependency.

As noted in chapter 1 there are several factors which impacted on a country's level of development and a reduction in the level of poverty, crime and

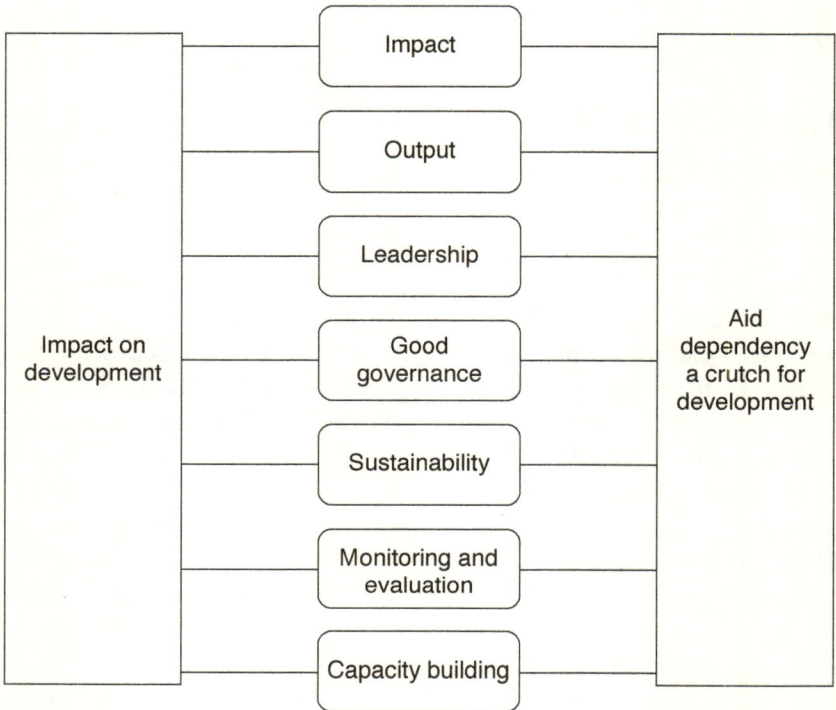

Figure 4.1. Impact framework
Source: Walters (2015)

violence. These factors include five major categories – historical, political, economic, social and environmental – which have had significant influence on the impact and outcomes of these projects.

These challenges have, however, raised several questions regarding the attainability of development and the true meaning and representation of development for people residing in these beneficiary EU PRP II communities. Development is seen as a difficult multilayered progression of economic, social, political, environmental and cultural change, which results in an increase of the wellbeing of people and extends their rights and choices without compromising the facilities of future generations to enjoy these benefits (Sutton 2005). Real development, however, is the procedure whereby individuals and societies build their ability to encounter their own needs and advance the quality of their own lives (Durning 1989). Physically, it means identifying solutions to the basic necessities of food, access to water, adequate clothing and shelter, access to basic healthcare, education and employment. Socially, it means developing the institutions that can promote the public good and restrain individual excess; and individually, it means empowerment, increased self-respect and self-worth (Durning 1989).

Another challenge that has impacted this discourse is the issue of quantity versus quality. The EDF 10 provided €8.5 million over a period of seven years to ensure that the PRP II goals and objectives were achieved (EC 2004a). However, the quality of the aid provided is determined by the degree to which the development dollars were distributed based on the needs and priorities of these PRP II communities (EC 2004a). This perception varies depending on the lenses through which they are seen. While the European Union felt that it had fulfilled its mandate, communities contacted felt that the projects were not based on their needs. This was also evident because in the focus group discussion, members of the community had to be reminded of the aid provided before they were able to comment, which is indicative of the impact that these contributions had on their development.

The Contribution of PRP II to the Development Discourse of Jamaica

The European Union is the largest grant donor to Jamaica with advantages that have had unparalleled impact on the GOJ's development agenda. This is as a result of responsive and efficient structures organized by the GOJ for the absorption and disbursement of these funds (Moncrieffe 2010). One of the most impactful projects is the PRP II programme that was designed to contribute to and support fifty-two poor and marginalized communities in Jamaica. Non-state actors and government agencies were to be included to encourage communities to prioritize practical poverty-reducing activities for implementation (EC 2004a). Under EDF 10, the focus on poverty alleviation remained, and included justice and security as focal areas, focusing on the engagement of civil society in crime prevention initiatives; understanding of the criminal justice system; and enriched outreach programmes for victims and perpetrators over the period 2009 to 2013. Despite the change of political administration in 2007, there has been a comprehensive continuity of overall policy direction by the GOJ (Moncrieffe 2010). However, the international financial crisis and lack of credit availability brought about an involuntary change in approach in terms of re-engaging with and entering a new IMF programme, which had not been on the country's radar. With these factors at the forefront, the development landscape shifted in an attempt to address some of the immediate restrictions and identified gaps (Moncrieffe 2010).

Various evaluation reports revealed that participating organizations in PRP II developed good practices that were strengthened though project execution. JSIF's administrative procedures also minimized possible corruption practices, facilitating greater transparency, accountability and participation in project delivery. Greater collaboration with government agencies such as the Rural Agricultural Development Agency, SDC, police, academic institutions, the church, the Jamaica Agricultural Society, the correctional services, other international agencies and local members of parliament was encouraged. This participation and collaboration also fostered greater cohesion among the sectors and raised knowledge of the guidelines (EC 2014). The support from the EU PRP project increased advocacy, training and research, which has allowed for success in enhancing development programmes such as the Jamaicans for Justice (JFJ) programme. The European Union has also assisted JFJ to further observe the Human Rights Convention through strengthening the role of civil society in the promotion and protection of human rights – a mandate of the UN Declaration of Human Rights in the advancement of a country's development. Based on the PRP II contribution, the work of several NSAs has also been reinforced through EU thematic programmes (Moncrieffe 2010). Prior to the call for proposals, efforts were made to check with civil society organizations working within the thematic area at the country level. Responses from these organizations then informed significant areas for funding, although problems were experienced in dealing with social and economic risk factors, which aided as knowledge points for contingency planning, project assessment, logistical planning, monitoring and evaluation. Similarly, there were reports of amended administrative skills, as well as report writing and financial management. However, the question of project sustainability has been raised. Preliminary findings indicated that in many civil society organizations, human and financial resource constraints existed, which could impact staff retention and capacity (Moncrieffe 2010).

The methodology for aid distribution as previously presented has proven to be effective. This is seen as more aid donors have adopted some of the principles and practices of EDF 10 to encourage greater accountability and transparency. Therefore, the gap between aid and development success closes only when aid is made accountable to its intended beneficiaries, which would mean institutionalizing accountability to the poor in development agencies. For this to be achieved, it requires great support and involvement from all stakeholders and encouraging the dispossessed to participate in planning and decision making. It may be difficult to measure the success of this, or its contribution to development, because results might not always be in a tangible measurable format. However, it would have the ripple effect of creating and fostering an environment of greater transparency and accountability, which are major milestones in the fight against corruption and in the establishment of good government structures.

It did not appear that the European Union and JSIF found working with these communities easy, because the root problem was often the intense clash of cultures between the bureaucracy – the European Union and JSIF – and the vision of the community groups. Operating in a destitute community where local informal political structures have to be constantly navigated and there are issues of continuous modification, uneven primacies, and short-lived opportunities, working relations are established not on contractual obligations but on mutual trust. The resulting clash of cultures leaves both sides resentful and discontent, making it difficult to quantify and measure development because the communities often feel that their true needs are not being met and the access to the aid provided is limited. In addition, it appeared that the implementing agencies also considered their role to be minimal and undervalued. The creative energy and commitment of implementers is wasted in filing reports and stifled by arbitrary planning periods. However, financial and organizational co-operation is particularly important to help local actors in working out sound development projects. Despite the many challenges and the debate around PRP II involvement in the development discourse, it is important to remember that countries such as Jamaica have flourished on the provision of aid provided by agencies such as the European Union and much of our infrastructural development and technological advancements are as a result of the contributions made from EDF 10.

Difficulties with the reach and scope of the aid provided should not detract from the fact that the benefits derived from the EU grant funds have advanced our reach toward true development and allowed us to achieve a number of our developmental goals. However, not all of the contributions provided can be measured or the benefits quantified. Questions also arise when the basic needs of the people are not being met and the nature of the aid provided is only short term, so the project ends with community members lacking the capacity to sustain themselves without continued aid, thus unable to achieve the development goal.

The Role of Communities and Community Development in the EU Project Management Discourse

1. Community and Community Development

Investing in people's hopes, dreams, goals and improving their lives are premised to be at the centre of development. The EU PRP II agreed with this model and engaged a total of fifty-two communities with the primary focus being youth inclusion, community safety and NSA capacity building.

2. Profile of Design and Results of Grant Actions

According to Vincent (2009), a community is defined as the interaction among people with shared interests who reside in a particular area, or a collection of people with collective interests. However, Bartle (2003) pointed out that a community is a social construct, not necessarily a tangible location. Instead, community can be a common interest among people, such as persons who identify with the LGBTQ community.

From the interviews, it was identified that the definition that best suited these projects was people having a shared interest or lived experience and having been identified as being vulnerable, or fitting into one of the thematic areas for poverty reduction established by the European Union. It is expected that the projects will lead to community development and empowerment. Vincent (2009) described community development as a process whereby all citizens are involved in community change and improvement is linked to the ABCD approach that highlights the practice of community development as a people-centred process. Remenyi (2004) also noted that development is both a process and an outcome – a process of growth based on self-reliance and contentment, which will result in development and empowerment of community members. This relies heavily on participation, community capacity development and sustainability, the increase and maintenance of which are challenging. Community members should take ownership of these projects and their needs and concerns should always be taken into consideration, but sadly this is not always the case.

3. Community's Involvement

One of the main means of increasing project success is to encourage involvement and boost community participation. Participation, however, has several levels – individual, public and social – which do not operate in isolation. Each level has stakeholders that the DFID defines as "any individual, community, group or organisation with an interest in the outcome of a programme, either as a result of being affected by it positively or negatively, or by being able to influence the activity in a positive or negative way" (2002, 21). The involvement of stakeholders is important to the revitalization of communities and is needed to encourage community buy-in of PRP projects. One respondent from the elite interviews said:

> My recommendations would be more abstract as to community involvement. I believe the key first step could be the communities need to organize themselves and that requires a huge investment in terms of time and money from even the people. I have always thought of it as unfair since some communities whose residents seem to

be more economically stable organize themselves and get certain things done whilst the other communities, because they are considered underserving then they get this treatment. (Elite interview, April 2014)

Heck (2003) argued that involvement of the poor in small groups encouraged their empowerment. Through their groups and organizations, they not only access resources, but also secure decision making and bargaining power and create a base for sustained self-development efforts.

There exists a quandary with regard to stakeholder's participation and the impact it has on development. According to Pretty et al. (1995), the quandary for many development agencies is that they both need and fear community members' participation. There is a perceived need for people's agreement and support and also a fear that this involvement is hard to control and will have an adverse impact on planning and implementation. This fear results in participation being observed in theory and not in practice. Shepherd (1998) noted that community involvement is usually asserted, not demonstrated. If community members' participation is translated into practice, it could encourage individual and public empowerment with people being able to partner with each other to assist in identifying glitches and requirements, organize resources, and assuming accountability for planning, managing, controlling and assessing the individual and collective actions that they themselves had decided on (Brett 2003). Oakley (1991) reiterated this point because she believed this involvement would develop skills and abilities to enable rural persons to manage and would provide them with a voice in negotiating for future development systems. This is further reinforced by Eade and Rowlands (2003) who argued that powerlessness is a key component of poverty, and any concentration on poverty, inequality, injustice or exclusion comprises scrutinizing, challenging, and changing power and power relations.

Community involvement can further be broken down based on typologies and levels. These typologies include: passive contribution; participation in information given to people; participation by consultation; participation for material incentives; functional participation; interactive participation; and self-mobilization. Typology has been used by the European Union to incorporate community members in the project cycle. This proposes that involvement in the planning and decision-making processes is representational. Hickey and Mohan (2004) argued that what is considered involvement in development projects is a procedure whereby large numbers of people are characterized by a relatively small group of participants. While Blair (2000) supported this view, he also cautioned that even though indigenous representation may be set up, the real "power behind the throne" often rested externally. Response mechanisms from communities may also present another problem, as project activities approved for execution may reflect only the welfare and priorities of the minority community leaders and not those of the entire local communities that they represent.

A respondent from an elite interview elaborated:

> They use quite a bit of what they call community based contracting where up to a certain level the community is a community group that is contracted to do the labour and the services. And that is seen as part of the capacity building process. . . . I that how it is meant to in a sense, it need to be properly evaluated and whether community based contracting or work, what do you do for things like training and all? (Elite interview, April 2014).

It is at the stage of project execution that the majority of community members "participate". Community involvement in this stage was said to be through the utilization of unskilled labour during various construction works, contribution of cash, involvement in various training programmes and actual execution of programme activities. Such participation is an example of "participation as contribution". This form of participation has shown some traits of "coercion" as community leaders enforce some sanctions and penalties on community members who do not contribute voluntarily (Oakley 1991; Dale 2004).

Despite the European Union's efforts to try and encourage community development there are, however, several obstacles that they are faced with, which can be divided into three categories: structural, administrative and social (Oakley 1991), usually typified by a top-down development approach. Administrative obstacles result because of the bureaucratic procedures stipulated by the guidelines and the adoption of a blueprint approach, providing little space for people to make their own decisions or control their development process. The guidelines also stress a standardization of approaches (Guijt and Shah 1998) that challenges the primary aim of participation and community involvement. According to Cooke and Kothari (2001) participation is translated into managerial "toolboxes" of procedures and techniques. This provides insight into numerous critical paradoxes: project approaches remain concerned with competence and focus attention only on visible, formal, local organizations, overlooking shared activities that happen through daily interactions, and socially fixed arrangements that may impact on the building of trust among community members. Dale (2004) also identified other obstacles such as power arrangements within indigenous communities; rigid professional attitudes among programme and project staff; little awareness among people of rights they may have or opportunities they may exploit; successfully conveying to local residents other stakeholders' involvement and support of the process; educating residents about the goals of the project/process; and the capability to communicate technical information in an easy to understand manner.

4. Community Capacity and Qualification for the Successful Implementation of EU PRP II

An important criterion for encouraging project success is an understanding of the climate that exists within these communities, especially with regard to poverty, unemployment, environmental issues and crime and violence. To access the EU PRP II grant funding, it was important that communities experience one or more of these vulnerabilities. The poverty-environment link is one of dynamism; reflecting geographic location and scale, and the social, economic and cultural characteristics of individuals, households and social groups (World Vision 2002). With these issues at the forefront, Jamaica, as part of its national development strategy for sustainable development, has attempted a prioritization of issues and unemployment, crime, poverty and environmental management have been identified as the most pressing (Andreasson 2010). This is seen as being in alignment with the PRP II programme (PIOJ 2007). According to the PIOJ (2007), 14.8 per cent of the population lived below the poverty line, having decreased from 35.2 per cent in 1992. Despite this significant decline, the incidence of poverty remains a problem for the country with a high concentration being in rural Jamaica. The poverty map of Jamaica identifies the parishes of Portland, Clarendon and St Elizabeth as areas with the majority of their populations in the poorest on the poverty index. The 2002 parish report elaborates further with St Ann, Trelawny, Clarendon, Portland and St Thomas having the highest incidence of poverty for the period (PIOJ 2012).

For communities to access the EU PRP II grants, they were required to mobilize into organizations and participate in the implementation process by contributing human or capital resources. But for this to be achieved, having access to social capital was critical. Dale (2004) noted that the livelihoods of peoples in developing countries are tied more closely to the physical environment, where there is greater dependency on the countries' natural resources to improve the standard of living of their citizenry, particularly in rural areas. Bhargava (2006) noted, however, that communities lacking in natural resources often faced challenges such as access to potable water, adequate sanitation facilities and suitable infrastructure. One of the main concerns is the eradication of poverty and providing access to these resources, often important to achieve the social capital needed to attain development: "When project communities galvanize or sections of the community galvanize and sometimes the leaders of the project becomes the object of a kind of cynicism, that is bad for the community overall, because people may think that for example they personally benefited from funds that were granted for the projects. That was not so in reality but people perceive it to be so" (elite interview, April 2014).

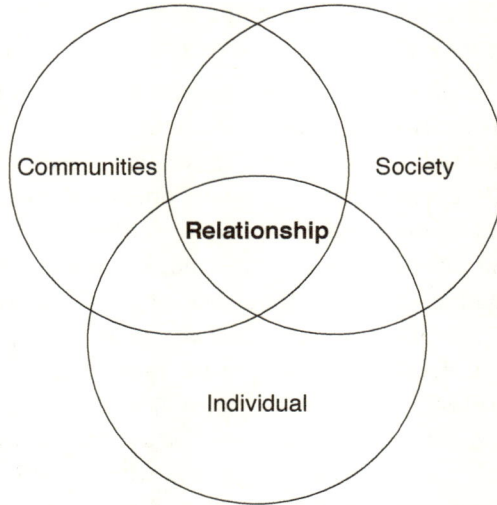

Figure 4.2. Intersectional model for community success and development
Source: Walters (2014)

A link exists between individual expectations and capacity at the community level. This linkage also impacts on the country as presented in figure 4.2 that shows the intersectional model that highlights the relationship that exists between the individual, the community and society, and the ability of the community to mobilize itself using the resources that are accessible to them. Each element is interconnected and does not operate in isolation. The model highlights how this has contributed to the discourse.

At the individual level, community members are seen as human resources and their value or worth is predetermined, based on factors such as access to basic services, education and employment. The relationship level highlights the relationship that exists between individuals in the personal space – which is also translated into the public space. This is the relationship among community members. As stated in the focus group discussions, a community with good relationships and a cooperative spirit will be better able to achieve project success. These communities as a unit encompass several features such as poverty, the prevalence of criminal activities and unemployment, which hamper their ability to achieve the social capital needed for project success.

Communities are able to mobilize their own resources to execute community expansion initiatives through community funds, revenue collection, selective exemptions from local levies and private sector funds. These resources are supplemented by the influence of labour, time and other inputs, particularly enabling the direct involvement of most community members. The communities' greatest asset is dependent on two things: its human capital and access and availability of resources. This is further manifested at the societal level that reflects the quality of institutions in the given country, the access to resources, the efficiency and effectiveness of government structures:

> So we look at the results of the evaluation and say well this seems to have been going correctly and meeting the objective but in fact at our last meeting with the presentation of a report from consultants on a small project done through NGOs and so forth, it showed that there is a fair level of success which was as a result of the community being able to galvanise. (Elite interview, April 2014)

The ability to mobilize and the availability of financial and other resources to the community has been effective in maintaining sustained improvement on the quality of life. However, poverty is a major bottleneck and can only be improved if the efforts are sustainable and meet long-term needs:

> The beauty of the programme is that the community contribution does not have to be in cash, it can be in kind. So that's one positive about it; but if it is that we find that we need more money we can't at the eleventh hour increase the grant; once the grant has been given that's it. So it means that the community now has to find more, and that more that they have to find is not in kind, its cash. (Elite interview, May 2014)

All contributions should be adequately recognized and accounted for. There should be mechanisms enabling the communities to recognize their own contribution and efforts made to reward their input, because for many community members this is a huge sacrifice. Figure 4.2 highlights the possibility for community sustainability based on the relationship that exists between donor and receiving communities. This yields both individual and community impact.

5. Community Empowerment through Project Participation

The primary objective of the project is to encourage poverty eradication and community empowerment using "JSIF as the primary implementing agency that invests in community based projects as a means of empowering communities and building social capital" (PRP 29th EDF/JM9c-01-2007-2011). This reduction of poverty should be visible. According to Sen (1999), poverty eradication can be assessed in five dimensions: political space, economic space, social space, transparency and protective security. If poverty reduction is not achieved and reflected in these dimensions, there will be a negative impact on the ability of people to improve their competencies and purpose as empowered persons. Poverty reduction, broadly defined, involves procedures that help people expand their competencies and functioning structures, which enable people to take charge of local affairs instead of being petitioners before higher authorities (Sen 1999).

The EU model aims to create such processes despite the fact that greater participation and inclusiveness is needed from community members. Community empowerment is unsustainable when development is driven by donor funds. It needs to be entrenched in the institutional framework of the local governments through harmonization with political, administrative and fiscal elements that need to be supported by the head of government to work out legal and constitutional arrangements (Sen 1999). Communities will be truly empowered only if they receive unencumbered grants that empower them to adopt their own priorities and improve their decision-making skills with greater utilization of the bottom-up approach.

The intent of the EU PRP II was to help empower local communities in areas with high levels of poverty to shape their future by giving them more resources and the authority to use these resources to improve their standards of living. Empowering communities is a critical and smart approach, and is a key part of effective poverty reduction strategies reflected in the EDF 10 mandate. However, several scholars have put forward definitions of what it truly means to empower a community and there are varied definitions and discourses around the word empowerment. Rocheleau and Slocum (1995, 4) defined empowerment as a "process through which individuals, local groups and communities, recognise and shape their lives and the society in which they live". They also noted that it is a "measure of people's capacity to bring about change, which is concerned with analysing and addressing the dynamics of oppression and assisting groups and individuals to play an active role in the decisions which affect their lives". In the context of this study, the main agents of community empowerment are the people, and for this change to be achieved, it means that they are able to organize and influence change on the basis of their access to knowledge, to decision-making processes and to financial, social and natural resources that contribute to their social capital. Perkins and Zimmerman (1995, 569) noted that the process of empowerment was an "ongoing process by which people gain control over their lives, democratic participation in the life of their community, and a critical understanding of their environment". The definition indicates that the main drivers of the process are the individuals that form part of the human resource base, therefore, empowering them through consciousness raising is critical to the empowerment discourse. Developing their capacity and knowledge will provide the confidence and knowledge for them to want and establish change, which helps with the success and sustainability of the projects, creating and fostering an environment for greater impact.

Community empowerment by definition is a collective rather than an individual process. Therefore, the objectives must be shared between the members of the community. Participation, relevance and reach of all members must be achieved. From the focus group sessions, it was highlighted that communities can be organized quickly and productively to diagnose local problems, come up with solutions, and lay down priorities and action plans that can be used to strengthen community organizations and accountability. However, for this to be achieved, the members of the community must be educated, and empowered with resources and authority. This was reiterated several times in all focus group discussions. Based on the module used to engage the communities, it is required that they form an organization following the guidelines presented. That body would symbolize their effectiveness. However, a primary criticism of the model is that the community organization constitutes a small fraction of the community, unable to represent the needs of all, therefore voices are lost and the concept of empowerment is distorted. Several of the respondents to interviews and focus groups indicated that in this situation, outputs did not equal impact because the needs of many had not been represented, therefore no empowerment had been realized.

PRP II was able to achieve its objectives as the infrastructural projects stipulated for parishes were completed. Twenty-five civil works projects in volatile communities had been approved for funding for an estimated J$510 million (EC 2014). Most were infrastructural, deemed to be "sexier" when reporting, as these are easier to quantify and showcase. For example, in the parish of Clarendon, infrastructural work was done to the Effortville Basic, Primary and Special Education Unit; similar infrastructural improvement was done in Kingston and St Andrew and other parishes and upgrades were carried out on a number of police stations and courthouses. The question, therefore, posed as a follow-up in the interviews was, "Has this approach contributed to the development success?" Many of the respondents felt that it did not assist with achieving development or aid in empowering individuals or communities because it was felt that the work done was not sustainable. An example was given of a police station where upgrades to the bathroom were carried out as the project used to empower that community. However, when the space was visited by one of the implementers two years after the project ended, she found damage to the facilities – the toilet was broken and window panes were missing. This alludes to the fact that the objective of empowering these communities is structurally flawed, and shows several weaknesses that must be addressed to encourage project success and sustained development for true empowerment to be achieved.

Challenges of Using the Guidelines as a Promise for Aid Development

The arguments centred on aid development have been very controversial because different discourses are presented using the guidelines to achieve project and development success. Aid can be considered beneficial and has positively impacted economic development and brought about improvements in the quality of life for many Jamaicans. But, at the same time, it has also had negative effects on some of the very outcomes the European Union had hoped to encourage, such as policy ownership, fiscal sustainability, institutional development, and, ultimately, autonomous long-term economic growth. Aid is supposed to provide temporary financial assistance in order to encourage certain long-term behaviours (Moyo 2009). As suggested by the focus groups in communities who benefited from the PRP II programme, this was not always achieved because the needs were often not met. For example, a number of the communities felt that their direct needs were not being addressed. One community related that the:

> VTDI is near to us and all of these things but not everybody have the five and how much CXC subject. HEART [the Human Employment and Resource Training Trust/ National Training Agency] also requires you to be able to pass the entry test so you have to have a Grade 9 level education. VTDI is mostly bachelors and degree programmes and so forth, and most of the guys in the community if I can speak for them, they maybe go up to 9 or 8 or whatever; they maybe can pass the entry test but they don't have the subjects. (Focus Group 2, May 2014)

The respondents from this focus group spoke passionately of the need to access education to encourage employment, therefore increasing individual and community wealth creation. Despite being one of the communities to benefit from the PRP II programme, they did not feel that what was provided was helping their development. Their most pressing identified need – acquiring certification in the required subjects – was not being met, denying them the opportunity of improving their quality of life, an important feature of development.

Another theme that arose in the assessment of development was the ability to build capacity in the community (which is further discussed in chapter 5). In some cases, the lack of progress in this area was attributed to political instability in both the formal and informal structures of leadership. However, the guidelines do not recognize the informal leadership structures that exist, which has a bearing on the implementation of these projects. Members of the communities are engaged, especially in developing countries with, according to Reno (1998, 8), "the emergence of warlord rule in the context of the collapse of the central state".

For example, two of the communities identified in the PRP II programme were political rivals and it was stipulated that both these communities needed to share resources for the project: "Kintyre is one community and Highlight View is one community. We are what you call a garrison community then, right, and Kintyre is also a garrison community; so you not going to expect the guys to stray to a next community for fear of their lives, you understand" (Focus Group 2, May 2014).

The result was that people from Highlight View opted not to engage for fear of their lives, hampering the success of the programme for the beneficiaries from that community, and resulting in the failure of the project. In this kind of scenario, the informal structures of leadership need to be acknowledged based on our cultural context. This does not mean that they should be celebrated or acknowledged as correct instruments for operation, but recognizing their existence and making plans with the reality in mind would help in achieving project success and development. This is a critical component to the discourse as this speaks to the ahistorical mechanistic approach that needs to be considered, and which was neglected in the development of the guidelines, even as the discourses surrounding the political and cultural environment was a theme presented that formed part of the narrative surrounding their use.

In addition, there are costs associated with aid-related organizations, practices and procedures in the current EU aid system. These comprise a long-standing and well-known list of shared grievances about aid such as volatility and ambiguity of aid flows; fragmentation of donor efforts; project proliferation and duplication; and conflict between donor and implementers' agendas (Bräutigam and Knack 2004). For instance, from the interviews, the point was reiterated that the creation of donors and projects constituted a significant burden for the small number of qualified public officials, who spend their time attending to donor concerns and managing aid activities rather than encouraging the development of the country, which sometimes resulted in implementers losing sight of the bigger picture. One of the concerns raised during the interviews was the lack of expertise that exists locally with regard to EU procedures and guidelines, and reliance and reference was made constantly to one person, the project manager from JSIF – as the key person who could provide support. In addition, reference was made to the online support and ease of access to persons at the European Union to provide clarity on issues that may arise while using the guidelines during implementation. From the earlier discussion, some of the flaws associated with using them and the implications of these discourses on the community and on parties who engaged with the text and the associated challenges were demonstrated.

Although governments normally criticize the conditions, they still find it easier to accomplish their goals by meeting the donor demands, than by increasing taxation. The large aid flows release them from the need to justify their actions in order to secure public support, but have the effect of increasing their dependence on aid. This, when added to indigenous resources, means the flow of revenues to the state is not affected by government inefficiency, encouraging governments to underinvest in developmental capacity. Heller and Gupta (2004) also argued that aid created a moral hazard because it reduced the incentive to adopt good policies and reform inefficient institutions, and thus weakened the government's developmental performance and encouraged rent-seeking and other means to achieve development. However, Stokke (2009) pointed out that the MDGs can be achieved by increasing the amount of foreign aid. Rostow's stages of economic growth also underlined the importance of initial capital for Third World countries in following the development path of industrialized nations (Stokke 2009). He argued that aid can provide capital and facilitate technological transfer through technical assistance. Aid can be capital or technical assistance that can be used as a catalyst for development (Stokke 2009).

Inputs in the Development Discourse: The Effect on Output, Outcomes and the Impact on Jamaica's Development Goals

Despite the millions of dollars received for development assistance each year, there is still very little known about the actual impact of DFID-funded projects on the poor and underprivileged residing in these identified communities. There are, however, broad assumptions and projections being made regarding GDP, economic growth, investments in human capital and the provision of safer communities for the poor. It is difficult and almost impossible to state that these positive changes were as a result of PRP II. However, the assumption is made that if good project management tools and practices are employed then there exists a positive correlation. This is further explained when closer attention is paid to the PRP II result chain, which incorporates the use of key project management practices such as input, process, output and outcomes, which all translate to the impact that the project will have on the communities.

Developing indicators that track these varied components will help in determining whether an activity is being executed as planned, if it is leading to a reduction in poverty, crime and violence, and whether it is essential to adjust project activities to maximize benefits and overcome unanticipated obstacles. Without data on inputs, activities, outputs, outcomes and impacts,

Input	Process	Output	Outcome	Impact
↓	↓	↓	↓	↓
• Money • Human resource • Infrastructure • SDC community profile	• Procurement of equipment and services • Construction and fixing of building and other infrastructure • GOALA & NABA project approval process	• Tangible & intangible • Executed funded GOAL and NASA projects • Constructed and improved buildings	• Better infrastructure • Example: Lucea courthouse • Basic schools infrastructures improved	• Poverty alleviation-> with an inclusion for Justice & Security and an emphasis on civil societies in crime prevention and better understanding of the criminal justice system
↓	↓	↓	↓	↓
Input	Activities	Output	Outcome	Impact

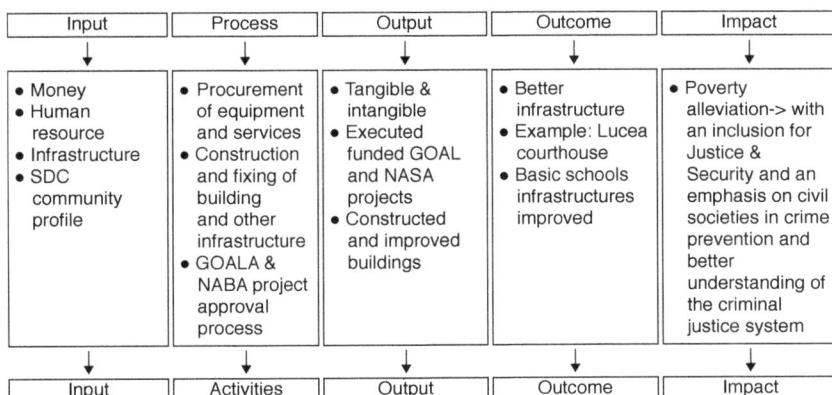

Figure 4.3. The PRP II results chain

Source: Walters (2015)

it is impossible to distinguish between poverty alleviation projects that are achieving their intended benefits and those that need to be modified or shut down. This is further examined in the PRP II result chain in figure 4.3.

The PRP II results chain highlights the five crucial elements of project success: inputs, activities, outputs, outcomes and impact. For the purpose of this study, inputs are the raw materials and support provided by the DFID to alleviate poverty. This includes human resources, grant funding and the encouragement of participation and involvement of the community in the implementation of the projects. These inputs are further translated into activities, which are based on the attempts of DFID and JSIF to meet project objectives. These include the facilitation of project grants to GOALA and NSA projects, the procurement of goods and services, construction and rehabilitation of buildings and other infrastructure. These inputs and activities help in the manifestation of outputs and outcomes that can either be tangible or intangible benefits that the project intervention is designed to deliver, such as the rebuilding and rehabilitation of a number of buildings and other infrastructure to aid in the alleviation of poverty. This approach is further debated alongside impacts. It is easier to iden-tify outputs or outcomes of the project as higher-level development goals but the impact of the project is sometimes neglected because it is seldom thought out at the implementation stage.

The development discourse emphasises that greater attention and focus be placed on the role of impact in project success. UNDP (2005) defined impact as the longer-term results of a programme – technical, economic, sociocul-tural, institutional, environmental or other, whether intended or unintended.

The intended impact should correspond to the programme goal. This definition can be further expanded to include the OECD interpretation that posits that impact is "the totality of positive and negative, primary and secondary effects shaped by a development intervention, directly or indirectly, intended or unintended" (2000b, 30), which means that not all project impacts will be immediately visible or need to be planned for. The same can be said for PRP II. From the midterm evaluation report produced by Tienhoven (2009), the overall objective had been defined as poverty alleviation through sustainable growth. Although there was no direct contribution foreseen to create sustainable economic growth in the target communities, the PRP II activities are said to have led to improvement in this regard because it laid the foundation for future economic development and sustainable growth (Tienhoven 2009).

In addition, PRP II is said to have created improvement of basic infrastructure for education, which speaks to the outcome and output of the project. This output is seen as having a long-term impact on the community because this improved future employment potential for the youth of the targeted communities (Tienhoven 2009). Also, improvement of basic road access to the target communities is also seen as having the potential of raising the profile and value of the community, which would also increase its attractiveness for future economic development. However, as mentioned in the elite interviews by a number of respondents, this was not the case because the main challenge with such infrastructural development was their maintenance and sustainability, since the communities lacked the necessary resources for this. Therefore, while these impacts were all represented in theory, there was no correlation in practice. Another main objective of PRP II was increased institutional capacity of the CBOs to facilitate the acquisition and implementation of future projects to stimulate economic growth within their communities. However, several arguments will be presented further on in this chapter on the ability of PRP II to develop capacity, since participants in both the elite interviews and focus groups felt that capacity development was not achieved.

Recreation and leisure spaces are premised to have a positive impact on the lives of members of the community (Williams and MacIntyre 2001), therefore an improvement of facilities such as community centres and schools to provide facilities for after school programmes should result in enhancing the social capabilities of youth through increased integration and interaction with each other, leading to a reduction in crime and violence (Williams and MacIntyre 2001).

However, it is difficult to state if this was achieved in the targeted communities, or if the youth were able to transition into the employment market. Finally, an improvement of support structures for volatile and vulnerable communities through strengthening entities such as the SDC and selected NGOs should have increased the opportunities for positive future development of the communities. Therefore, while it can be surmised that the PRP II contributed to the development discourse, the extent of the impact and the sustainability for economic growth depend on the communities' own commitment toward further development and on the supporting opportunities provided by public institutions and NGOs.

Sustainability, equity and competence have had a direct impact on the output and outcome of the project, and a robust link with the type of institutions governing the execution. The European Union's involvement is critical in dictating these parameters. However, neither the European Union nor by extension JSIF as the implementing agency, operate in isolation, so achievement cannot be solely attributed to them because there are other variables that impact on this success. Figure 4.3 is an analysis of the attributes that assist in realizing project impact, which further translates into development success.

The impact analysis measures the valuing of change that can be attributed to an intervention. This means that it is not enough to say that the PRP II project objectives or goals have been met, but the degree of success that can be attributed to that project must be determined. That is, "the extent to which observed development effects can be attributed to a specific intervention or to the performance of one or more partners taking account of other interventions, (anticipated or unanticipated) confounding factors, or external shocks" (OECD-DAC 2000a, 1) must be assessed. For PRP II, the challenge is to draw conclusions on the cause-and-effect relationship between the different sub-projects and the reduction of poverty, crime and violence. As seen in the chain model presented in figure 4.3, it is difficult to assess a linear model of change, because one examines the flow of the results chain, from outputs to outcomes and impact, thereby making it difficult to attribute intermediate and long-term results (outcomes and impact) to any single intervention or actor. As there are several factors that may arise that are sometimes not just unique to the culture of the country, but unique to the culture of the community, the standardization of the model in the initiation and implementation of the project needs to be taken into account when assessing whether or not that intended impact was achieved. Impact can be translated differently depending on the communities, and the intended benefits and outcome will produce different impacts. As highlighted in the focus group discussions, some communities might be more receptive than others.

Another critical point to note is that these communities are a flourishing garden of aid projects and programmes throughout the year. Therefore, it is difficult to attribute any success to one project or programme. For example, the building of national capacity may be as a result of several projects and programmes both locally and internationally. However, the exploration of partnership as a means of strengthening the likelihood of the achievement of development goals and affecting the reach and impact of these projects through resource and goal sharing, will widen development results.

Environmental and political factors also affect the impact of projects. Based on geographical location, there are certain issues that may affect a project's effect on development, such as hurricanes and seasons of drought. In the political sphere, there may be informal political structures, and different agendas or priorities that may arise with a shift in ruling political parties. One party may view poverty alleviation through more "soft projects" as its main concern, while another may favour "hard projects" to reduce crime and violence as the approach needed for greater impact. However, although PRP II like most DFID projects was heavily infrastructure-based, from the elite interviews, it appeared that more "soft projects" such as parenting training would have had greater impact on the communities.

Many people in the elite interviews raised the issue of the inability of the implementers to follow through with assessing the impact of projects on the communities. They were of the view that it was usually easier to conceptualize and measure output indicators, as impact indicators could be multifaceted, expensive and problematic to measure. Also, the time lag between programme execution and impact could be significant, because impact analysis required understanding the processes of change in the wider context (Roche 1999). Despite efforts being made by the European Union regarding monitoring and evaluation of the projects, a deeper assessment is needed, such as before and after household and community surveys to collect comprehensive impact data for ex post evaluation. However, the time and cost they require make them impractical as tools for monitoring or evaluation during project execution.

The Role of Sustainability in the Development Discourse

Any aid programme is challenged in its ability to satisfy the human needs and aspirations of all its beneficiaries. The immediate basic needs for a vast number of the people in developing countries are food, clothing, shelter, education and employment opportunities. These are not always met and if they are, it is often only for a short time – specifically during the project period. Nonetheless, these individuals have legitimate aspirations for an improved quality of life. The best way to address this is to first acknowledge that we operate in a world in which poverty and inequity are endemic and will always be prone to ecological and social conditions that foster a cycle of poverty. However, the situation can be improved through sustainable development that focuses on the basic needs of all, and extending to all the opportunity to satisfy their aspirations for a better life.

According to the World Commission on Environment and Development (WCED 2002), sustainable development is defined as growth that meets the desires of current generations without impacting the ability of future generations to meet their needs. It comprises two key concepts: needs, in particular the essential needs of the world's poor to which priority should be given; and limitations, imposed by the digital divide and the social environment's ability to meet present and future needs. For the purpose of this study, sustainable development may be seen as incorporating three important but different elements: (1) balance – which focuses on the trade-offs needed between social, environmental and economic interests; (2) equity and shared responsibility – extended over time and space to meet a greater number of individuals with special consideration to addressing these needs for a longer duration; and (3) participation – as greater involvement from beneficiaries and all stakeholders will encourage greater sustainability as all voices and needs will be brought into the discussion for holistic decisions.

It has been argued that the attractiveness of the concept of sustainable development lies in its elusiveness (Redclift 2005). Its indefinability has been purposeful because the main concern has been to drive through a broad agreement or to attain a minimum guarantee to some broad understanding of change. The European Union recognized that having a "one-problem, one-indicator" approach that aimed to develop a framework that tried to bring the economic, social and environmental aspects of society together was needed to encourage sustainability. Thus, the PRP II sustainable development plan was divided into three main areas of focus: institutional sustainability, sustainability of infrastructure sub-projects and sustainability of personal development. As presented in Tienhoven (2009), the sustainability measures implemented by PRP II were expected to be good because most programme activities had a sustainability component developed during the planning and implementation stages.

At the institutional level, PRP II focused on four institutions as part of the sustainable development plan: JSIF, the SDC, the MNSJ and CBOs. As noted in chapter 3, within the PRP II, except for the MNSJ component and the construction of the Lucea Family Courthouse, JSIF was responsible for the management of all programme components, and in particular for the implementation of the sub-projects. JSIF's general institutional sustainability focused on staff development because it was intended that a number of the staff involved in the implementation of PRP II would continue to work with or for JSIF beyond that programme, and, having accessed this knowledge would provide additional support and expertise for future social investment initiatives. Additionally, they would have gained knowledge of the management of social development projects because the guidelines provide a detailed and comprehensive overview of the basic principles needed to successfully implement most development endeavours.

Another partner in the implementation process was the SDC. Tienhoven (2009) noted that the institutional sustainability of the SDC could be taken as guaranteed because several recommendations had been made to develop its capacity and raise its profile. However, any investments required for the improvement of its facilities and services depended on the identification of "external" financing sources, such as PRP II (Tienhoven 2009). Elite interviews with SDC representatives suggested that not enough was done to encourage and guarantee sustainability of the organization. The general sentiment was that they were not seen as equal partners; although PRP II expected a great deal from them, their involvement at the planning stage was more on the back end.

It has been presented that the sustainability of the MNSJ was raised. Based on the involvement and the structure of the MNSJ component through the CSJP, which is financed by a loan provided by the IDB, it was felt that the CSJP was not sustainable because this was not considered a regular department with inbuilt structures that would promote sustainable development. At the community level, it was felt that the structure that was put in place strengthened CBOs that were involved in the implementation of sub-projects. In addition, CBOs that were selected usually had a track record supporting their sustainability. Their further continuation and development were often dependent on the engagement of one or two key personalities. However, in this context it is also a general observation that in similar programmes, key personalities "leaving" one CBO will most likely join or establish another one in the same community. As a consequence, even in these cases, the capacity improvement facilitated by the programme will remain within the community, thus encouraging sustainability (Tienhoven 2009).

Living standards were sustainable only if consumption principles spoke to long-term sustainability. However, many beneficiaries lived beyond these needs. Perceived needs are communally and culturally determined, and sustainable development requires the elevation of values that encourage consumption standards that are within the bounds of these possible prescribed needs. The sustainability of sub-projects manifested in the maintenance training that CBOs received, a standard component of JSIF's sub-project implementation procedures, was one medium used to achieve this. However, several arguments have been presented regarding the sustainability of a number of these infrastructural development programmes as noted in the elite interviews by a number of respondents. They felt that much of the infrastructure was not

maintained despite having a maintenance component built into the implementation process. For example, school buildings, which represented most of
the sub-projects, should have had their maintenance and sustainability facilitated by the Ministry of Education's general support to schools; and by parents'
associations, which in most cases had indicated their willingness and capability to handle this. However, this was not achieved in all cases because funds
were often shifted from this area to meet immediate priorities that arose, thus
promoting the vicious aid cycle and the continuous restart to development.

An expansion in numbers can increase the pressure on resources and slow
the rise in living standards in areas where deprivation is widespread due to
the lack of distribution of resources, interest and leadership. For example, in
community centres, experience has shown different levels of commitment
from CBOs. Some make every effort to take care and maintain the facilities,
while others experience leadership changes over time, resulting in the neglect
of maintenance activities. Consequently, compared to school buildings, their
sustainability is less assured, in spite of JSIF's efforts to select responsible CBOs
based on their commitment and track record. This often results in the dete-
rioration of community centres that return to a deplorable state, in need of
great repair and assistance. "So the projects can only add to the sustainability
of the community if the structures were in place to make it sustainable" (elite
interviews, May 2014). Therefore, a society may in many ways compromise its
ability to meet the important needs of its people in the future – by overex-
ploiting resources, for example (Tienhoven 2009).

> I have recognized that the EU is doing more and more in terms of what is called
> sustainable livelihoods to ensure that what is done with the EU resources are inter-
> ventions that could help people improve the quality of life by the old adage "giving
> a man a fish is one thing but teaching a man how to fish is another thing". And I get
> the impression that the EU is more and more helping countries and communities to
> learn how to fish and not giving them a fish. But at the very local level, I think maybe
> more could be done in terms of ensuring sustainability of its interventions. (Elite
> interview 6, April 2014)

Meeting critical needs depends on achieving full growth potential, sustainable development, and economic growth in places where such needs are not
being met. Economic growth provides the bases for growth which replicates
the principles of sustainability. But growth by itself is not enough. High levels
of widespread poverty can exist, and can impact development. Hence, sustainable development requires that societies meet human needs both by increasing
productive potential and by ensuring equitable opportunities for all.

Another way of encouraging greater sustainability is by placing greater
emphasis on soft projects such as activities that support the personal

development of children and youngsters, always with the objective of improving their chances for future integration into the labour market, and deterring their joining the local gang scene. These activities, generally accepted as an appropriate approach, facilitate improved school opportunities for young inhabitants of volatile hotspot areas (Tienhoven 2009). This objective would have been better met with greater collaboration and coordination with other programmes and projects, which take over once the school education is finished. The personal development facilitated by PRP II activities (which also include those activities planned within the MNSJ-managed component) could be more sustainable, if they were better coordinated with services financed and provided by other organizations, and with other PRP II components. "We have such a culture with financial resources and the needs especially for capital development in the country. Our ability to sustain that is rarely tied to the ability to earn as a country. Unless we are able to earn our way out of the predicament that we are in the short answer is it is not sustainable" (elite interview 5, April 2014).

Sustainability, equity and efficiency, and effectiveness are the fundamental requirements of any region-based resource programme (Tienhoven 2009). The programme needs to be sustainable on the grounds of output, impact and institutionalization. The sustainability of the organization rests on the involvement of the stakeholders, especially the beneficiaries of the programme at the time of planning and through its execution. Equity needs to be interpreted from the viewpoint of direct beneficiaries as well as benefits to indirect participants. Efficiency and effectiveness involve achieving anticipated outputs and impact with the preplanned unit cost of the programme. Growth has no set limits in terms of population or resources. The accumulation of knowledge and greater understanding of the impact of the development discourse on Jamaica's development can enhance the carrying capacity of the resource base. Jamaica must encourage and ensure equitable access to the constrained resource and reorient efforts to relieve the poor so as to have positive development advancements.

The Role of Capacity Building in the Development Discourse

Poverty is, beyond question, an issue most discussed on the development agenda at the international, regional and national levels. One of the prescribed cures is through capacity building and development. In the 1990s, the concept of capacity building became one of the priority areas for development theory and practice. International donor agencies have appropriated the concept. In fact, it has become the norm in development practice, which suggests a great level of consensus among interests, views and approaches.

But capacity building is also debated as being meaningless jargon that confirms the methods of contestation about conceptualization and operationalization that underlie development (Tienhoven 2009). Fowler (2002) defined capacity as the measure of ability, whether knowledgeable, structural, social, political, material, practical or financial of an individual, group, organization or community to achieve its objective. Capacity building would therefore be the answer to the absence of the ability, and can be understood as a set of technical interventions or processes aimed at individuals, organizations or communities to empower and improve their development (Fowler 2002). The EU capacity-building approach is concerned with support to numerous implementing organizations and communities required to respond to the multidimensional processes of social change. However, it is not only a responsive strategy. It also seeks to enable implementing organizations and communities to proactively shape these processes of social change for community development.

Figure 4.4 showcases the different roles of JSIF as implementing agency in the implementation of PRP II. JSIF is expected to have the capacity for project management, service delivery, operation and management infrastructure, implementation, policy, institutional and national development.

As discussed in previous chapters, the EU model is designed to assist beneficiaries of the projects to work out their objectives. The approach worked better in some communities than in others and provided the support for strengthening the ability of the community to build structures, systems, people and skills and to better define and achieve its objectives. Developing community capacity enabled members of the community to identify and utilize the skills and resources they needed to take control and improve their lives, and to encourage greater sustainability of the PRP II project, while providing an empowering experience.

The discourse around capacity building and its contribution to development can be categorized in five thematic areas: (1) improving stakeholder participation; (2) increasing problem assessment capacities; (3) developing local leadership; (4) building empowering community organizational structures; and (5) improving identification and mobilization of resources. From the data, it was identified that these five themes represented the European Union's influence on the community programme's political, sociocultural and economic capacity.

Capacity building originally embraced the left-leaning range of intellectual and political traditions, but this approach has shifted and is used to further a neo-liberal agenda of self-involvement – according to Eade (2010, 89), a "pull-yourself-up-by-your-bootstraps kind of economic and political agenda". However, this postmodern approach to capacity development can result in the guidelines becoming insignificant, or at worst creating damage, as communities try to drive their own empowerment without the knowledge and training

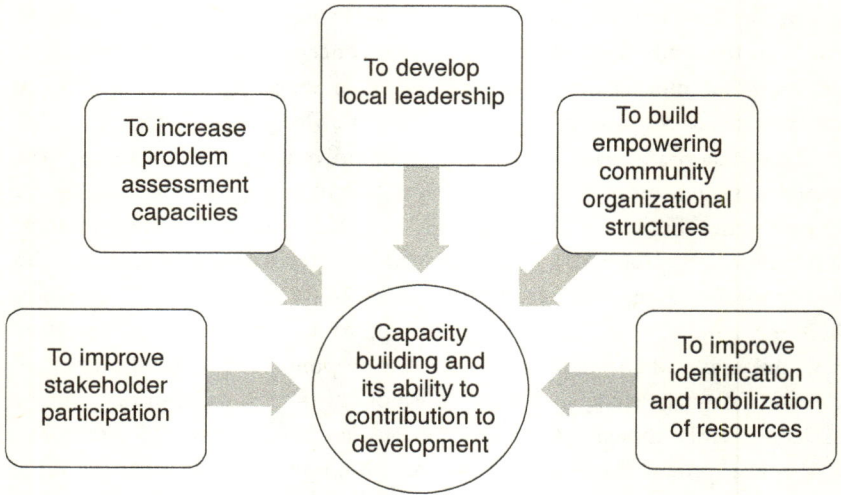

Figure 4.4. Capacity building and its ability to contribute to development of local leadership

Source: Walters (2015)

needed to identify and utilize their resources (Eade 2010). Eade also posited that capacity building is not a commodity that can be concentrated to a set of ingredients for a universal recipe on "how to do it", but, recognizes that there are several diverse and competing actors in development that will impact the success of the project (Eade 2010).

The danger also exists of developing a reliance on the European Union, an engaged outsider, to support the capacity of local people to determine their own values and priorities; to organize the communities through the assistance of JSIF; and to act upon and sustain the moral and physical environment of these communities to further the development agenda. The key indication that capacity building had occurred was the presence of improved structures and competences in place to carry on the work of the NSA after a grant-funded action was completed. The Medium Term Evaluation Report for the PRP II proposed a similar standard for sustainability of PRP II interventions (Tien-hoven 2009). Against this background, three major groups of outcomes arising from investments to improve the capacity of NSAs were identified – positive changes in the productivity, scope and results of the operations (Bell 2012).

The implementing agency supports the EU agenda for development so it executes all plans through partnership, with one unit acting as a silent partner and the other assuming the lead role. This relationship is manifested in the operationalization of the acceptance and use of the guidelines. In order to

encourage and support the development of the staff of the partner organization, JSIF, and build its capacity, autonomy and power, one would need to get
out of the driver's seat and learn to hone navigational skills during the planning
and implementation of the project. But the reality that exists is that the European Union as the donor agency has the power and "he who has the money
rules", thus limiting the level of involvement and growth from both JSIF and
the SDC. This has a ripple effect that also affects the community because it is
clear that one cannot build capacities in others that are not evident in oneself,
and if one cannot learn then one cannot teach. However, the creation of structures is a mechanism that was established to combat this and expand the reach
of operations in communities.

This idea of capacity usually refers to an organization as subject, hence its
close ties to the operations (Biggs 1999). NSA capacity in this analysis arises
from their means to process activities, and interventions that modify this
capacity that influence their ability to organize, design, develop, implement and
monitor activities, as well as to adapt to structural changes in the economy and
society. The project sponsor also gains project development and implementation experience that raises the profile of the organization. This capacity-building
approach is haphazard and is not necessarily streamlined based on objectives.
For example, once the NSA undergoes a successful project process, the organization would automatically have developed project management skills that can
be used for further social development projects. This type of capacity-building
outcome is passive and regarded only as residual capacity-building gain, for
example the parent subgroups formed in Kintyre, August Town and Whitfield
Town by three grantees. In each of these cases, the subgroups were rolled into
the broader outreach efforts of the NSAs, which were mainly churches. Other
examples of residual capacity structures include business units, and individuals
who were originally cases under the long-term psycho-social support of NSAs
(Bell 2012).

Capacity building is an approach to solidarity-based partnerships with a
variety of expressions. For example, in terms of the business units, clusters of
small business operators were established in Canaan Heights, Bucks Common
and Effortville in Clarendon; and in Dunkirk, August Town, Kintyre, Tower
Hill and Jones Town in St Andrew. The business activity included agribusiness
sectors such as bee and ornamental fish farming, which were expected to make
these communities self-sufficient. The sustainability, longevity and applicability
of these projects is questionable and their ability to raise the capacity of the
community members has sparked several debates. The focus group discussions
with three of these communities revealed that the goal was not achieved as the
identified general needs would first have to be met in order to achieve capacity

development. It is important to remember that there is no quick fix to development; this insight was mentioned in the elite interviews by several people. For example, while attendance in workshops raised knowledge and capacity of individuals in the community, there were still basic needs that would first need to be addressed to facilitate access to this knowledge. For instance, consideration and contingencies would need to be put in place for transportation of participants to the venue and for the provision of food to facilitate the learning process. These additional needs are not always budgeted in the project costs and will not always be seen as priorities (Eade 2010). In addition, if these communities are going to be viewed as equal partners in the quest for true development, then the approach would need to entail mutual accountability, including accounting honestly for decisions that affect others. This approach is challenging and time-consuming, demanding flexibility, shared risk-taking, open discourse and a readiness on both sides to respond to feedback (Eyben 2006).

Collaboration is further encouraged at the grassroots level. An example of this is the Rastafari Youth Council Initiative that developed a partnership with the Jamaica Business Development Cooperation for the first time during the PRP II project, to provide important resources to the grant-funded action. Similarly, Public Display of Action engaged private sector expertise to deliver grant-funded technically-intensive activities in the fish farm installation. These cases demonstrate the NSA's development experience for project design and administration in a multi-institution context, as the boundaries, reach and scope of the organization are expanded. These structures created a reference point for NSAs that are community-based and networked into a value chain and rolled into their resource base to support organizational development, such as occurred in August Town, where the NSAs and stakeholders were equity and profit-sharing partners in the business operation.

The wealth created provides for consolidation of the business interest and community outreach activities (Bell 2012). However, there have been successful cases where the scope of operations was an outcome, with additional structures established to continue activities started under the PRP II grant funding. This was the case in Brown's Town and Kintyre for actions that involved two NSAs, and multiple communities in the case of another NSA. More specifically, one NSA started honey-making as an income generating activity, while another started fish farming. Despite the successes, the reality is that most development aid has little to do with capacity building of the poor to enable them to alter their societies. Not even the best-intentioned aid donor is exempt from the tendency of the development industry to ignore, misinterpret, displace, replace or undermine the capacities that people already possess (Eade 2010).

A capacity-building approach therefore means getting out of the world where projects have clearly stipulated start and end dates, and concentrating less on secondary scores of projects and more on seeing social interventions at the local, national, regional and global levels. Training may be successful in its own terms, but may contribute very little to empowering participants to modify their realities. Translating these successes into sustainable changes in people's lives means listening to them, and a long-term commitment. Rather than viewing support community activities in a fragmented or insular fashion, the aim should be for a more holistic experience. A change in one part of the system may have negative repercussions on another part; therefore, some structures involve a planning cell that would serve as a point of contact between communities, and between communities and the NSA, which would anticipate difficulties and address them when they did arise.

This mechanism was used in a sports promotion that involved One Hundred Lane and Park Lane, two unplanned communities close to Red Hills Road. The same structure was used in Windsor Heights (Central Village) between as many as five districts but this generated different results (Bell 2012). "In terms of capacity building I believe it was really limiting. SDC provided validation and verification in terms of the designs which were done but it was limited. In some special cases some projects focused on some civil training however generally it was limited" (elite interview 3, April 2014).

The general consensus from all sources of data such as the elite interviews, focus groups and reports was that there was a need for more to be done to ensure capacity building and development of all stakeholders in the successful completion of PRP II. At the community level, there were mixed feelings about the knowledge gained and the capacity raised, but it was felt that a basic understanding of their need would have assisted in making a greater impact and in further developing their capacity.

The Role of Community Leadership in PRP II on Community Development and the Development Discourse

Leadership has played a fundamental role in the implementation of PRP II both at the organizational and community levels, each with its own leadership structures and challenges. Effective leadership within the community is needed for the achievement of project goals and to complete successful community actions, encourage social well-being, and improve community viability. According to Gardner (1990), leadership is the process of persuasion used by an individual (leader) to encourage an individual or group to pursue objectives held by the leader. This is evident in the approach administered by the European Union for the implementation of social development projects such as PRP II. It is assumed that effective leadership will encourage greater community development, assisting the beneficiaries of the project to become more competent and gain some control over local conditions. This should result in greater sustainable community development that is needed for the achievement of true development. However, this cannot be achieved merely through shared will or coercion. Instead, a greater collaborative effort is needed by all participants to share their ideas, visions and responsibilities equally and democratically in steering and implementing their community development projects. A group of people to drive the process and to facilitate a smooth transition needs to be identified.

Leadership, a key agent in successful community development, is an engaging process between individuals within a common locale (Goeppinger 2002). Without it, efforts may be made to execute poorly conceived programmes (Sabran 2003). During the implementation of PRP II, there was heavy reliance on CBOs and their presidents because they formed the backbone of a number of these communities. This registered during the focus group discussions as these individuals were often held in high esteem. References were made to their vocality, intelligence, knowledge and sometimes education. Their role in liaising between agencies of development and their communities stood out clearly as they were often the nexus between the community, the implementing agency and the funders. Wilkinson (2005) noted the importance of these community leaders because they usually had a direct impact on the life and well-being of their communities. They also filled prominent roles in community action, many working to develop the common good of their community, thus making them agents of change.

However, a concern was raised during the elite interviews about the selection process for a number of these CBOs because it was noted that in some communities, the executive bodies comprised only family members. This nepotistic practice has had a negative impact as other community members have refused to get involved, thinking that any benefits would be shared among a select group. In other instances, leaders who worked toward positive outcomes were also discouraged and demotivated as they felt that community members were disinterested in the activities, so consequently their needs and interests were not being met. These negative nuances resulted in a reduction in participation, thereby limiting the impact and reach of some of the PRP II projects. This reinforces the need for effective leadership at the local community level in order to harness the will of the people to work toward their own development. Changes in PRP II communities' structure affected not only the social construction of the groups, but ultimately the social capital and community leadership as well.

The role of formal and informal leadership structures needs to be considered if development is to be achieved. Community leaders, governments and organizations should be viable partners in the development discourse and the goals and objectives for the community need to be shared. The success of any development project depends on whether it has good monitoring and evaluation approaches (James 2014), as these are essential to making prompt adjustments during the project life to ensure compliance with targeted objectives. Respondents noted that neglecting to highlight and address the concerns mentioned earlier led to the failure of many development projects in their communities.

Access to social capital is also essential to the development process. One of the major roles played by indigenous leaders in the study was the identification of resources for community development. This was often surrounded by conflict as communities were not always satisfied with the way previous projects had been executed and may have opted not to assist in the process that would have facilitated the community being qualified for future aid.

Community leaders were also expected to bring about change in the communities, where there was need for greater access to education and employment opportunities. However, community leaders expressed concern in the focus group sessions that community members seemed more interested in handouts, and they spoke of several challenges trying to mobilize attendance for meetings and training sessions.

Contributions by community organizations and representatives such as CBOs are invaluable to the development discourse, based on their provision of social capital and voluntary services. Agencies such as JSIF, CSJP and SDC rely heavily on their ability to mobilize communities and disseminate information. They acknowledge that they cannot depend solely on power and formal authority to accomplish things, but, as Pigg (1999) observed, community leaders must depend on networks, influence and specifically the relationships developed through extensive interactions within the community to influence people toward a shared goal for action. Ahmad et al. (2014) suggested a community development model as a viable option because this framework was more collaborative and comprehensive in nature. The model utilizes a participative kind of leadership, whereby community leaders involve community members in the early stages of programme planning and also in its implementation.

The Need for Monitoring and Evaluation for Project and Development Success

And people don't understand that just doing some things could actually be counter to the very objective that you have, if you don't monitor and evaluate at the impact level.
(Elite interview 7, May 2014)

From the data collected and presented earlier in the chapter, it was recognized that there was a challenge with measuring the impact of PRP II on the fifty-two communities that it tried to empower through poverty alleviation. This was as a result of incorrect monitoring and evaluation strategies employed from the projects' initial stages to the closing stages, with no clear purpose in mind perceived. Monitoring and evaluation should be undertaken with a range of purposes in mind. These should include measuring impact, outputs, efficiency, effectiveness or change; strengthening accountability; facilitating organizational learning so as to encourage capacity building; and encouraging the sustainability of project outcomes so as to enhance project success.

According to the World Bank (2011), monitoring is a continuous function that uses systematic collection of data on specified indicators to provide management and stakeholders with ongoing development intervention, progress and achievement of objectives and progress in the use of allocated funds.

Measuring changes in people's lives is a key aspect of monitoring and evaluation. When monitoring activities are undertaken correctly, the following objectives will be achieved:

1. identification of shortcomings at the beginning of the development and ensuring they are addressed in timely manner;
2. monitoring the development of the entire project; and
3. ensuring changes in the context and circumstances of the implementation of a rapid problem identification system as well as a system for internal communications to all stakeholders (Singh and Nyandemo 2004).

If these objectives are achieved, there are greater chances that the project will be successful and increase the likelihood of the achievement of development goals. In this way, the ultimate aim of development, human rights and activism is achieved – that is, to bring about improvements in people's lives.

However, during the implementation of PRP II, development targets seemed narrowly focused on measuring outputs as opposed to assessing impact and sustainability. There is no need to reinvent the wheel, instead, the rights-based monitoring and evaluation approach could be adopted, measuring a wide range of indicators. Practical experimentation with different monitoring methods and indicators is key to developing essential skills and to making the choices that have the greatest impact on the realization of people's rights. More emphasis is placed on needs and empowerment of the target population, which will lead to greater impact and sustainability. In addition to changes in people's lives, emphasis is also placed on changes in accountability, equity and participation (Singh and Nyandemo 2004).

A change in the responsibility of duty bearers can be made more real by evaluating changes in policies, use of the EU guidelines, laws, resource distribution, and variations in attitudes, values and practices. However, it should always be remembered that changes and modification to the guide, laws and policies do not automatically translate into improvements in the lives of poor and exploited people. It is therefore necessary to monitor changes made to these instruments as well as changes in people's lives and the development of the community.

Monitoring plays a key role in the community development process. According to Casley and Kumar (1987), the primary aim is to provide funders, implementers and other stakeholders with regular feedback on the progress during the implementation. The feedback from monitoring projects can be used to better inform key decision makers, the public, as well as other stakeholders. However, the system must supply the project management with a continuous flow of information throughout the course of the project to make it possible to take the right decisions. There needs to be a continuous process of collecting and analysing data to compare how well a project is being implemented against expected outputs and impacts. Monitoring of community development projects is a challenging exercise. The main challenge lies with the monitoring of the information. While this is necessary, it is however not sufficient input to the conduct of rigorous evaluations (Casley and Kumar 1987).

Although monitoring information can be collated and used for ongoing management purposes, depending on such information on its own can present misrepresentations, because it covers certain dimensions of the project's activities, and careful use of this data is needed to avoid involuntary behavioural incentives. One method of handling it is to rely on monitoring information to identify possible problem issues requiring more comprehensive investigation via an evaluation. However, this approach also has its own sets of challenges as seen during the implementation of PRP II. A key observation expressed in the interviews related to the midterm evaluation which was done by a European consultant (Tienhoven 2009). A number of respondents raised concerns regarding the validity and reliability of the report, which was a problem commonly faced in the Caribbean. Because of self-reporting and monitoring, donor agencies have considerable influence on the outcome of the monitoring process.

Another challenge with the monitoring systems was its set of quantified physical and financial indicators, many of which are not entirely appropriate for social development projects because their outputs are not easy to identify or measure. This made it difficult to assess the link between the policy outputs and the production of desired impacts. For example, a reduction in crime is affected by many factors so it is extremely difficult to isolate the contribution of the PRP II project as the primary agent to any reduction in crime. Another challenge relates to PRP II's broad objectives and goals – the alleviation of poverty to encourage community empowerment and development. This is also difficult to evaluate and if success is achieved, it is difficult to correlate this success with a particular project because these communities are often the recipients of other aid intervention projects with similar goals and intentions.

According to Spicker (2008), projects are evaluated mainly by scrutinizing evidence in order to make some judgements. He argued that the first requirement for programme evaluation is the establishment of some sort of criterion by which it can be judged. Evaluation can be defined as a process by which general judgements about quality, goal attainment, programme effectiveness, impact and costs can be determined by the consequences of policy, programmes, or by looking at whether they have succeeded or failed according to a set of established standards. Therefore, the primary aim for evaluation, according to Theodoulou and Kofinis (2004), is a review of the entire project in order to assess its overall value and effects when completed. It is also an instrument to assist planners to initiate new projects and decide whether existing interventions should be supported or rejected, and to help the overall effectiveness and efficiency of social interventions – in terms of their outputs, outcomes, costs and impacts – and where necessary, determine the catalytic effects and sustainability of such projects.

However, the challenge arises when such information is not used for future projects, and lessons learned are seen as mere theoretical contributions. Therefore, the result is a negative impact on future projects because old mistakes will be repeated and little to no true development will be achieved.

The Impact of Good Governance on the Development Discourse

Good governance practices are needed to ensure effective and efficient project management and development success. Discussion around the applicability of good governance has been on the development agenda over the last twenty years and has become indispensable to the development process. The term was also introduced to the development discussion to focus on the role of the government in the development discourse as a medium to eliminate the negative effects of corruption and to encourage greater participation. Good governance is defined as "a process referring to the manner in which power is exercised in the management of the affairs of a nation, and its relations with other nations" (Kaufmann and Mastruzzi 2008, 3). In other literature, good governance is seen as "the traditions and institutions by which authority in a country is exercised for the common good" (Mastruzzi 2009, 103). This is needed to ensure that the management of economic and social resources for development is effective and efficient, and that there is transparency, accountability and popular participation by all stakeholders. Donor's aid intervention into the country is high, and with each intervention comes expectations that community empowerment and development are achieved, and that the only path is through political stability and proper management of public resources, all fundamental factors that have contributed to economic growth and sustained development.

In addition, PRP II's primary aim was the improvement of social standards and poverty reduction. However, while the government's role in establishing and maintaining governance structures has long been recognized, the role of the community in this process is also critical to the discourse. The ability to conform and adjust to the tenets of good governance is critical to enhancing the country's capacity to achieve sustainable prosperity, progressive economic growth and social development over a prolonged period. This largely depends on strategic decisions made about the allocation, investment and utilization of resources by all stakeholders in the development discourse. Unfortunately, the perception exists that it is the responsibility of only some key stakeholders to focus on the economic liberalization, globalization, privatization and market-centred reform that has been identified as the engine of growth, increasingly responsible for the creation and production of wealth, generation of employment opportunities, and the provision of goods, services and infrastructure. This mindset requires resocialization because *all* stakeholders, not some, are integral to the development discourse, and all need to be held accountable for the success or failure of each project. In fact, all stakeholders are responsible for the achievement and sustainability of these development ideals. Therefore, greater buy-in is needed from the community as active participants in the process for change, while the image of donors' development goals needs to be accepted by the community, as the main beneficiaries.

Corruption is a major challenge for most development plans because it undermines development activities and creates inefficiencies in the process. Corruption is also a hindrance to poverty alleviation because it expands the gap between the rich and the poor who are often marginalized and powerless. Corruption damages economic development, delays the growth of democratic institutions, and hampers the ability of developing countries to attract foreign investment. Therefore, commendations need to be made to the European Union as the rigidity and rigorousness of the guidelines used in the conceptualization and implementation of PRP II have managed to curtail acts of corruption. This was highlighted by a number of participants in the elite interviews.

For example, the area of procurement, the award of contracts to supply goods and services, has been identified as a loophole for corruption. A weak procurement institutional framework with disregard for or lack of understanding of procurement systems can result in mega corruption.

The European Union identified the procurement practices implemented in Jamaica as a major challenge and, with the PIOJ, adopted the following measures. First, procurement codes giving detailed rules and regulations had to be unified, providing for a transparent and competitive procurement process and avoiding the loopholes currently being exploited (EC 2004b). Next was self-regulation, through constant monitoring of activities to review existing internal control systems and decision-making processes so as to identify weaknesses. Additionally, the European Union has set up control mechanisms to enhance transparency and accountability, to ensure that these expectations are enforced utilizing the tenets of good governance (EC 2004b).

A common governance theme identified from the interviews was the issue of accountability of all stakeholders involved in the development discourse. Accountability is viewed as the responsibility of all stakeholders with each entity having a particular mandate (Shihata 1981). For example, it was the responsibility of the government under PRP II to allow room for flexibility during the implementation of the project. An example of this is seen with regard to procurement, because the EU procurement guidelines often took precedence over the GOJ procurement guidelines. In addition to accountability, there was the issue of responsiveness, since the project was expected to respond to the needs of the people, seen as tools in assisting the community with being empowered and achieving development goals. Also, participation was as a cross-cutting theme throughout the discussion on the contribution of good governance to the development process. However, these themes do not operate in isolation and all are needed to work together to create greater project success for the empowerment and development of the community.

Aid Dependency: A Crutch for Development

The 2009 Jamaica MDG report noted that the country had achieved Goal 2 (universal primary education) and was on track to achieve environmental sustainability and eradicate extreme hunger. The population affected by poverty decreased from 28.4 per cent in 1990 to 9.9 per cent in 2007; however, it rose to 16 per cent in 2009. Jamaica is currently one of the highly-indebted countries, and has been receiving IMF support since February 2010. It is now important to stimulate economic growth and create new job opportunities.

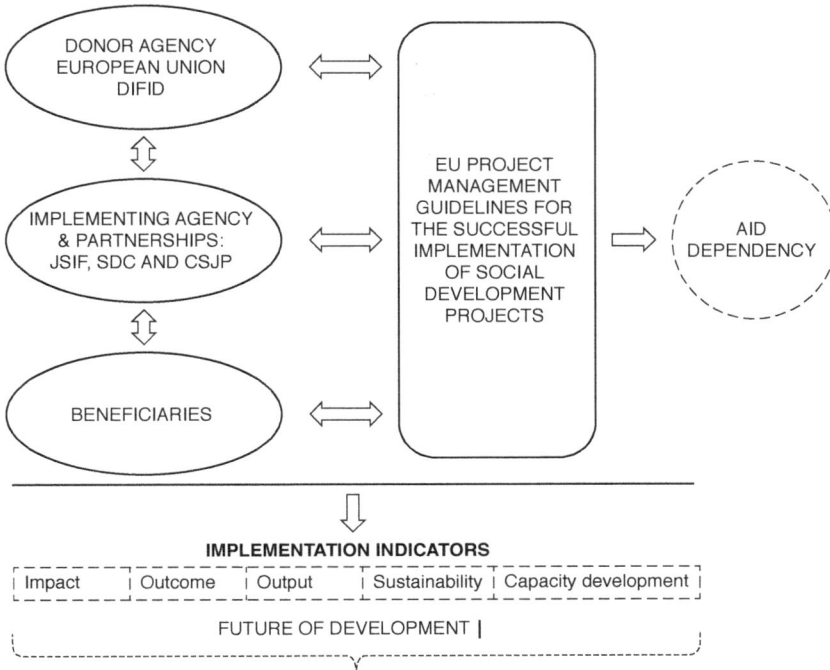

Figure 4.5. Conceptual framework demonstrating the linkage between the European Union as a donor agency

Source: Walters (2015)

As highlighted from the common country assessment, continuing high rates of crime, a public confidence crisis and civil unrest, which in May 2010 triggered a two-month state of emergency, demonstrated the need for governance reforms and an improved framework for addressing key developmental challenges (UNDP et al. 2011).

Figure 4.5 is a representation of Miles and Huberman's (1994) conceptual framework, which was used to demonstrate the linkages that exist between the European Union's role as a donor agency and the discourse surrounding its role in implementation. The diagram also shows the interconnectedness of the JSIF, SDC and CSJP roles in the implementation of PRP II.

Despite the challenges that exist with this partnership and the impact these various levels have on the beneficiaries of the community members, these varied elements represent the success or failure of development by showcasing the linkages between impact and outputs, sustainability of the projects and the level of capacity development.

One of the primary aims for the provision of aid through the EU PRP II was to reduce poverty and promote and encourage community empowerment and development. The manifestation and impact has sparked several debates and discussions among stakeholders with regard to the positive and negative impact on communities' development and empowerment. In addition, a culture of reliance and dependence has manifested in a number of these communities as a number of them have become heavily dependent on aid for their growth and development. The word "empowerment" is seen as the ability of persons to expand knowledge and control over personal, social, economic and political forces in order to take action to expand their life situations (Israel et al. 1994). It involves a process by which individuals and communities are provided with the opportunity to take power and act effectively in gaining greater control, effectiveness and responsibility over changing their lives and their environment (Fawcett et al. 1994). The key to community empowerment is the process or action that builds individual and community resources, and improves the efficiency and fairness of government structures, implementing agencies and beneficiaries of these projects. This is critical because proper management of the project and its resources will lead to greater effectiveness and efficiency of the aid provided.

"Development" and "aid" are often used synonymously since both are assumed to be the saviour for all social ills. Often, aid agencies assume that their priorities and objectives will naturally coincide with those of the beneficiaries of the programme. However, with the implementation of PRP II, this was not necessarily the case. As presented in chapter 5, there were conflicting viewpoints regarding what the community truly needed in order to reduce poverty and crime while fostering development. A detailed needs-based approach was required to identify project goals and objectives. In addition to this, some of the areas noted by donor agencies can be identified as highly politicized and agenda-based. This may actually crush the local capacities rather than releasing their potential, therefore having the reverse effect of disempowering rather than empowering individuals and communities.

The development industry in all its expressions is inherently self-serving. The pros and cons of international aid versus international capitalism may hinder social transformation that alludes to the cyclical nature of the approach used in aid development (Boateng 2009). The "good cop" international aid has also shaped government policies and made them more accountable and transparent to the people. In addition, the EU guidelines have minimized the practice of corruption and a number of individuals, families and by extension communities have benefited. It is critical to note that projects alone cannot change the future of a community or a country. The reality is that the beneficiaries of these communities are ill-prepared for the modern world, incapable of sustaining their community, and predestined to live even more marginally while waiting for the next group of well-intended visitors to show up with more project funding, thus fostering a cycle of dependency (Boateng 2009).

The underlying principle of empowerment is to provide these individuals and communities with a certain level of power, independence and autonomy. Lukes (1994) observed that power may occur at the individual, community and organizational levels. At the individual level, power denotes the ability to make decisions; at the community level, power implies that shared leadership and common decision making is achieved. Empowerment requires that power can alter and increase (Page and Czuba 1999). Empowerment is a procedure that promotes power, that is, the capacity of people to implement activities, for their use in their own lives, communities and society, by focusing on the issues that they define as important (Page and Czuba 1999). However, under the PRP II, while the communities were provided with the tools to empower themselves, the question arose as to whether or not power was given to these communities since this is significant to the development discourse. From the elite interviews and focus group discussions, it was revealed that while the communities were empowered to an extent, they still lacked the power to govern and make decisions that would directly impact their livelihood, and the general sentiment was that their development still lay in the hands of the donor agency and to a lesser extent the government. This is as a result of the fact that these communities still lacked the social capital and resources needed to be true decision makers and to have a voice in the development discourse.

Rappaport (1985) noted that all people have existing strengths and competencies as well as the capacity to become more competent. The failure of a person to display their ability is not due to shortages within the person but rather to the failure of the social systems to deliver or produce opportunities for competencies to be displayed or acquired. This was evident in the rigidness of the EU guidelines used in the implementation of PRP II because little to no provision was made to allow implementers to exhibit any level of autonomy in the administration of the project. In addition, as was noted in the elite interview, the guidelines do not provide allowances for beneficiaries of the project to effect their own change, grounded in an understanding that power will be seen and understood differently by people who inhabit various positions in power structures (Lukes 1994). Individuals and communities brought into focus another aspect of power that is characterized by collaboration, sharing and mutuality. According to Kreisberg (1992, 57), "the capacity to implement" is needed to allow for greater flexibility and autonomy of these community members through shared power that provides the opportunity for greater empowerment.

When this shared power is not realized, results are dissonant with the development discourse, which leads to an environment of dependency. Dependency exists when one party relies on another without the reliance being reciprocal. Dependency also speaks to a lack of self-sustenance and self-sufficiency. McKinlay and Little (1979) further elaborated that in such a relationship, one party may choose to terminate the relationship with little or no cost to them while the other can do so only at considerable cost. By this measure the recipient incurs considerable costs when aid is terminated. From the study, it can be deduced that aid provided by the donor (European Union) had a large amount of control over the recipients (fifty-two communities that benefited from PRP II). The demand for aid placed the donor in an advantageous bargaining position. The donors, therefore, dictated the conditionalities under which aid was supplied and the duration for which this aid was granted. The level of capacity and sustainability of the project was also dependent on the donor agency's perception of what was needed. Therefore, it had significant impact on the development of these communities.

Summary

The empowerment of communities in the development process is critical for true development to be achieved. However, underpinning the achievement of development is the discourse used to determine the success or failure of the project. The achievement of poverty alleviation and crime reduction are the primary focal points identified as being required to encourage development.

However, several concerns and challenges were raised as to the impact of the project on the community, the sustainability of the projects and its ability to develop the capacity of all stakeholders in the implementation of PRP II. The reasons for this were explored and concerns raised with regard to monitoring and evaluation exercises, because the projects were seldom given a detailed evaluation that looks at impact assessment to determine the effectiveness, efficiency, applicability and its ability to meet the needs of the participants. The need for proper leadership was also identified as being important for true development to be achieved. In addition, based on the discussions, evidence of a form of dependency on the donor country or other aid programmes is fostered and encouraged creating a discursive culture of aid dependency which acts as a crutch for development in countries like Jamaica. Aid then becomes necessary to provide citizens of the countries with the resources for their livelihood and daily needs.

5.

The North versus South Dialogue of the South Regaining Its Power

This chapter provides a comprehensive review of what was explored in previous chapters. The book provides a careful examination of the impact of the EU project management guidelines on development discourse, and the effect this has had on the intended beneficiaries of the project. Community empowerment is also discussed as an important theme to the development discourse. The discussion of a needs-based, bottom-up approach is seen as a fundamental component of this approach to encourage inclusiveness and participation of all stakeholders. The asset-based community development and rights-based community development models are also critical models that can be utilized and modified to our local environment to foster greater community empowerment.

The European Union was discussed, the impact it has had on foreign aid, and to a deeper extent, the culture of aid dependency. The role of language and the discursive agenda as a function for the rhetoric strategies used by the European Union was an essential component in its positioning and representation of voices. Social and environmental factors were also observed based on the mechanistic and deterministic impact they have had on achieving project success. The creativity employed by JSIF as the chief implementing agency was also discussed as a key element contributing to the discourse. The need for proper leadership was identified as important for the achievement of true development.

Second, the positioning of post-development theory as the theoretical framework was examined. The study is seen as an extension of the discourse around dependency theory, specifically, aid dependency. This is highlighted throughout with several illustrations of how the guidelines and other funding opportunities are used as a crutch for development.

Finally, the justification for the use of critical discourse analysis and the significant contribution it made to the development discourse is demonstrated. Critical discourse analysis gave precise accounts of how, and the extent to which social changes were affected using the development discourse and the relations between changes in discourse. Additionally, the non-discoursal elements and social life during the reconstruction processes of social change and empowerment in the quest for achieving development were also presented.

Discourse of Resistance

A positive or negative change or shift in development will cause a certain level of resistance as persons gain power. In order to empower communities against global discursive power, there needs to be a multimodal approach to community development and empowerment as seen in earlier chapters. Development discourse is made up of several elements and struggles at the political and ideological level. These criteria are represented and interpreted through various lenses and are heavily dependent on the stakeholders' position in the development discourse. This determines positions of power and levels of resistance, and ranks each discourse accordingly.

When the elements and struggles of the dominant stakeholder (the European Union) are identified, these ideologies become nodes in the discourse around which less important elements of the discourse are organised. The European Union and the implementers such as JSIF, MNSJ and SDC are key players in the process of recreating the development discourse. This institutionalized fixation of the central floating signifiers of development thinking, or the prescribed ideology of development, has been relatively stable, but the interpretation and enactment of this discourse have changed as donor countries such as the European Union reinterpret the meaning of these nodes while encouraging a structure that creates a particular ideology of what development should reflect. The utopian package of true development is held high as a benchmark to which each community aspires, but the prescribed text to assist with achieving this distant goal is seen as inefficient and ineffective, since true development is not standard. This in itself has led to greater resistance by implementers and community members as the forced ideology at times is rejected based on cultural discourses.

The basic discourse for development shows a state of closure as development aid is often provided for a short duration with each project having a start date and an end date. This approach raises questions of sustainability, impact and capacity building. It also raises concern around a community or country truly being emancipated and independent from the providers of aid, since development is guided by a global agenda to which these communities are forced to adapt. To alleviate this pressure would mean a resistance to donors such as the European Union that has rejected this ideology of development, and adjusting to the discursive environment, thereby creating a new discourse of multiple starting points and disengagement.

Resistance to any of the prescribed approaches to development is important, but the impact this resistance will have is heavily dependent on where the power lies. In order for there to be a shift in discourse, it means that those who possess the power must lead the charge. Therefore, adjustments are needed from the top and greater power needs to be passed on to implementers and community members to facilitate them being equitable partners in the development discourse dialogue. Resistance to these structures of operation would mean a reconfiguration or total reshuffling of these ideologies. Community empowerment through donor resistant actions against power becomes meaningful as parts of a resistance against the chain of equilibrium that is at the centre of the discourse. But the major challenge is that these communities do not understand the power they possess in making such an effective move for resistance.

North versus South Discourse and Its Impact on Western-Northern Hegemonic Relationships

It was observed that aid donors are powerful and overarching entities that effectively control a domain and influence the key agencies and the roles assigned in the development discourse (Evans et al. 1985). The concept of a dependent country may be regarded as a summation of the challenges faced by underprivileged communities, described over the years as weak, soft, underdeveloped, unlawful, underprivileged, inappropriate, rogue, collapsed and failed – each description attempting to capture one or a few problematic elements. As with other development concepts, dependent relationships are relative, but the impact that they have on the communities and countries that benefit from these programmes is sometimes overwhelming.

Some of the challenges identified included weak, ineffective, and unstable institutions; the inability to articulate community needs and recommendations to overcome these identified community challenges; lack of formal education to support themselves and the community; and lack of employment needed to assist in the mobilization of resources to make them independent. These challenges resulted in unstable and divided populations suffering from torn economic and social fabric; greater dependency on donor agencies for assistance to reduce crime and solve certain basic infrastructural problems; poverty; and low levels of economic growth and development. The result was a lack of capacity to fulfil basic functions of government.

It is not the intent of this work to accuse the European Union of being solely responsible for the creation of this dependency and disempowerment. But the relationship and the dependence on aid has mirrored that of dependency and has contributed to a number of the challenges previously mentioned. The current relationship and reliance on aid is manipulative. This was evident as priority areas or areas of weakness needed to be addressed to advance communities and provide them with access to basic needs and infrastructure to enable them to meet predetermined needs of the donor agency. However, based on the data collected, implementers and beneficiaries of the programme felt that too much control and too little room for creativity and initiative were provided, as their voices were not brought into the discussion and intended needs were not truly being met. This resulted in these stakeholders' feeling of vulnerability based on the restrictions of the guidelines and the penalties assigned for breaches. This vulnerability provided the donor agency with a means of control.

This control can also be interpreted as being burdensome and demanding, since this constant checking and over-involvement can disempower the beneficiaries of the programme. Autonomy is sometimes lost, as echoed by the SDC and JSIF. The EDF views this monitoring of their investment differently because they need to provide detailed accounts for funds disbursed.

There is also a tendency for a donor entity to believe they own what they control and ownership implies being able to do anything without accountability or consequences flowing in both directions – for example, the use of the procurement guidelines. The country's guidelines, as presented by PIOJ, are not always followed during the implementation of the project and the EU procurement guidelines often take precedence over GOJ guidelines during implementation of a project. Communities also feel this control as the resources they need for mobilization make them active participants in the process but without voices. Communities' assets have developed over time with the work of many people so they should be viewed not just as beneficiaries but also as stakeholders. Therefore, control is seen as having two levels: (1) the level of the implementation, with the relationship that exists between the implementers and donors; and (2) the community level, encompassing donor, implementer and community members who are beneficiaries of the project.

Another characteristic is the feeling of victimization. This is evident in some of the expectations placed on these communities to access basic infrastructure or meet some basic needs. Two communities in Jamaica were presented as examples. Both are geographically close but experience different socio-economic conditions. Interestingly, what was highlighted was the need by the poorer of the two communities to mobilize themselves into a formal organization and apply for a grant to provide access to basic infrastructural needs, while in the other community, similar requirements were not extended. Instead, they had access to basic requirements/needs, thus providing them with greater life opportunities to excel. This suggests a certain level of inequality, since those in the poorer of the two communities felt like victims. This feeling of marginalization is a common concern because it emphasises disconnect from community needs. However, attempts have been made to try and mitigate this through SDC community profiling. But based on focus group discussions and interviews, disconnect is still evident as the participants believe their needs were not being met. A rebuttal to this argument might be that applicants for EU grants are ill-equipped to complete the forms because of cultural discourses and level of education. This can mean disempowering moments for these communities while the process is being completed.

Power is important to the discourse of the relationship being dependent. A number of the arguments presented are as a result of the lenses through which the narrative is seen and the autonomy to write that narrative, which will determine the level of control and stakeholder's power, and the capability to limit the options of others. There needs to be a strong interest in breaking down this power and control in aid relationships. This can be difficult since the donor as the primary funder will always assume a position of power as the money-lender. Individuals who try to change a condition by articulating rather than acting are at a disadvantage when they are up against power and control. Taking action frequently results in retaliation, for instance, when an implementer seeks to make recommendations or changes in the guidelines as presented, the response can either result in support or punishment through penalties.

Contribution to the Development Conversation

From the previously raised issues, the author has developed a six-step approach, which is viable, to minimize the level of dependency by developing countries on developed countries. These steps work as a medium to encourage empowerment of all stakeholders and to achieve development by raising the profile of communities, providing them access to their basic needs and increasing their livelihood through greater capacity building and more sustained projects with greater impact:

1. *Assess the impact* of aid on countries' resources and members. This means to independently look at the true impact of aid and how this affects a country's economic and social growth holistically and individually. It is important to assess if aid has hindered or encouraged growth.
2. *Challenge viewpoints* of aid and assess definitions of what development truly means and costs. Throughout the study, several definitions were presented for what development truly means and represents, which are reflected based on the lenses through which it is viewed. It is important that we challenge these definitions and incorporate our cultural nuances to fit our understanding of both aid and development.

3. *Mobilize resources.* Communities in Jamaica are reservoirs of untapped resources. It is important that these are identified, mobilized and assessed as a part of the development discourse.
4. *Countries need to empower themselves.* There is a common concern that "power" is being taken out of empowerment in a number of these projects as a result of the restricted guidelines and the harsh penalties put in place. Therefore, it is critical that communities are empowered to maximize their true potential.
5. *Raise capacities and resocialize beneficiaries.* Greater involvement and trust will inevitably raise the institutional capacity of the implementing organization – for example, the use of local organizations and entities to assist in conducting monitoring and evaluation exercises. Resocialization of the beneficiaries will make them view themselves as more than just beneficiaries but also as key stakeholders in the development discourse.
6. *Increase sustainability.* A concern raised throughout the study is the inability of the projects to speak to impact, and the inability to ensure sustainability. Several examples were raised of buildings that had reverted to deplorable states when revisited. Therefore, greater attention needs to be placed on encouraging sustainable projects.

Greater project success and development will result if these six steps are integrated into project planning and implementation.

Putting the Power Back in Empowerment: Recommendations

Aid is not a panacea. It is one of several financial streams that flow toward developing countries. It must tackle the roots of poverty rather than its symptoms, and primarily be a catalyst of developing countries' capacity to generate inclusive growth.
(EC 2010, 4)

For development to be more than a façade, community empowerment is needed because both are interconnected. It is suggested that with modifications to aid conditions, this mode of uplifting communities can be seen as a viable option to assist with the achievement of development goals and encourage the implementation of successful projects. To achieve this objective, special emphasis needs to be placed on projects with greater impact, while outputs and outcomes are crucial to the discourse. It is important, too, that impact is seen as a critical medium of measuring the success of a project. Although difficult and expensive, resources need to be prioritized so as to encourage more impact assessment plans that shift the focus from project outcomes to more project impact. Additionally, this shift in focus can incorporate inclusive growth and sustainable development. As intimated several times throughout this study, sustained projects are critical to the development narrative. Therefore, a sustainable plan needs to be discussed and included in the initial stage to encourage projects to have greater reach, scope and lasting results. Development is not achieved until all involved are empowered, and one way of achieving this is through capacity building. It is important that implementers and beneficiaries gain knowledge and additional expertise to raise the profile of these communities. In addition to capacity building, emphasis also needs to be placed on strengthening existing governance structures and on greater facilitation of community leaders, so as to encourage a greater appreciation of what "development" truly represents in Western ideology.

Empowering Communities through Project Impact

The end result of any project should reflect the holistic long-term and short-term impact that projects have on the individual and on communities which they engage. This can be achieved by first mobilizing the community, by inviting members to dialogue and assessing their social, economic and political needs as tangible goals. If all voices are employed to raise awareness and create social empowerment attainable through rigorous monitoring and evaluation exercises, then projects should be more impactful. The creation of, and appreciation for partnership, are also critical to this process to minimize the effects of duplication. Ideally, a connection with past and present projects with agreed priorities is needed. This can be achieved through clustering projects along thematic or geographical lines as a means of encouraging interaction and broader dissemination of ideas.

A bottom-up approach is necessary for encouraging projects to have greater impact since community members need to be seen as stakeholders with voices in the process, with an interest in their own well-being and empowerment. If this is ignored, it will be difficult for a project to have any real impact on the lives of the people. In addition, this approach can be strengthened to promote greater project success with good governance practices, such as insisting that beneficiaries, donors and partners are accountable for development results. To facilitate the engagement of various voices in the dialogue, it is important that the European Union provides avenues to promote regular, structured and inclusive conversations to increase trust and mutual accountability among stakeholders.

A theme raised throughout the study is the inability of the guidelines to take into consideration cultural nuances and environmental uniqueness. It is imperative that the European Union invests in understanding the local arena and the cultural discourse so as to tailor its approach to better suit the needs of the community. If this is done, the process of implementation will be more adaptable and will eliminate some of the frustrations and disagreements that may arise due to cultural clashes – thus facilitating a more effective and efficient process. Adoption of such an approach will increase the likelihood of the project having a greater reach. Facilitating this process requires more openness on the side of the European Union. Its willingness to encourage knowledge transfer to build the expertise of implementers, to create a level of autonomy and independence, is a way of encouraging optimal utilization of the limited resources.

The human rights–based approach to development also needs to be considered to assist with projects having greater impact instead of using the asset-based approach to community development. Oftentimes, the community lacks the capacity and resources needed to spur it to request and qualify for such aid. Therefore, assessing communities based on mainstreaming human rights standards is a more equitable approach to levelling the playing field in the realm of new aid modalities. This requires an understanding of human rights in development, both as a means and as an end. This will impact the design, implementation, monitoring and evaluating of the EU aims and objectives to incorporate the five main principles of the human rights–based approach:

1. Accurate use of the international human rights framework;
2. Empowerment as a prerequisite for effective participation;
3. Involvement in development decisions;
4. Non-discrimination and prioritization of groups vulnerable to human rights violations; and
5. Accountability of duty-bearers to rights-holders. (European Union Action Aid 2008)

Regranting is another approach that can be used to resolve projects' impact. Currently restrictions delimit the amount of funding that can be distributed to any particular community and the time frame in which it should be used. If the regulations are revised, it will increase the flexibility offered for the provision of sub-grants, thereby allowing regranting to act as an effective mechanism to engage smaller organizations on the ground and strengthen their capacities. This approach could also be incorporated as an optional step in the project design and implementation because it would provide communities with the opportunity to decide if this step is needed. Some projects may need additional time and resources in order to have substantial impact on the lives of the intended beneficiaries (European Union Action Aid 2008).

Empowering Communities through Project Sustainability

Sustainable development represents a long-term change in power structures and community empowerment as important indicators for development success. As seen in previous chapters, this task is difficult to achieve and difficult to measure due to the fact that sustainability could take decades, despite being critical to the development discourse. However, the indicators to measure these changes need to be included in the project design and implementation. Indicators to measure empowerment may include, but are not limited to, measures such as community control and management of resources, as well as increased participation by beneficiaries of the project in decision making and administration of the resources that affect their lives (Binswanger and Aiyar 2003).

A project is seen as sustainable based on its ability to be effective, efficient and applicable after it has been completed. For this to be achieved, the European Union needs to draw from an appropriate mix of modalities and incorporate responses from all stakeholders with flexibility, open to the responses presented and adaptable to different local situations. This is to ensure that various nuances are incorporated in the development objectives in a more strategic, effective and sustainable manner. This approach will contribute to the strengthening of development aid effectiveness in the long term. The European Union must be more responsive and inclusive in developing its capacity and tools, to better understand the local contexts of poverty and crime – the main aim of PRP II.

An important component in sustainable project outcomes is it should be designed based on complete consideration of livelihood systems, needs and opportunities. Successful programmes should use bottom-up preparation to regulate priorities and then accurately reflect community needs in project design. This approach must identify not only the symptoms but also the root causes, including the systemic causes of poverty, the inequalities and injustices, as well as the victims and the most vulnerable groups so as to fully target the problem. Greater sustainability can only be achieved by taking a bottom-up approach, by focusing on the true needs of the beneficiaries of the programme and strengthening the local stakeholders' capacity to design a strong monitoring system that allows for the collection of relevant data to improve the project, making it more relevant and coherent to the ever-changing needs of the community. The fight against crime and poverty can only be won and sustained if there is continuous dialogue, participation, transparency and coordination amongst actors involved in the development process, including the poor themselves.

The primary aim of the European Union is to promote growth, not as an end in itself, but as an instrument for poverty reduction. For growth to occur, an effective sustainable plan must be built into the project at the beginning.

The European Union has to identify the main elements of the sustainable plan and determine how this will benefit the poor, acknowledging that there is no systematic causal-effect relation, and that poverty reduction cannot be approached with a one-size-fits-all strategy. A universal sustainable plan is not the answer. Instead, each plan needs to be tailored to take into account the cultural and environmental differences that may exist. It is also important to contextualize development action so that it matches the development needs and strategies of the beneficiary country. In particular, sustained efforts are required to improve the quality of life. Therefore, long-term, predictable and independent funding should be visualized to empower communities and more effort should go to improving the flow and quality of project deliverables in terms of accessibility and timeliness.

As already noted, sustainability must be deliberately addressed from the earliest stages of project design. This requires capacity building for all stakeholders and support for indigenous approaches to managing resources and conflict. To ensure the long-term impact of interventions, project designs should explicitly address institutional capacity needs and should actively cultivate effective capacity-building programmes for both the implementers and beneficiaries of the project. Developing the quality of JSIF is the key to improving its chances of being sustainable. Adherence to sustainable project design principles, where possible, is needed to build on both local and national implementation support systems as a means of minimizing recurrent costs and enabling the development of clear strategies. Sustainable project designs also create explicit linkages between the individual and existing projects to which they have contributed, and encourage greater community ownership by beneficiary communities, which is another critical factor contributing to the sustainability of project life and long-term benefits. Ideally, this is only achieved when participation is encouraged by the community along the entire life cycle of the project – design, implementation, and monitoring and evaluation. Community participation as an existing practice establishes community institutions. By building on existing community assets and knowledge, development agencies can promote positive community attitudes toward collaboration and collective decision making. They can also support social interconnection by strengthening relationships between internal and external organizations, thus making the effects of aid development relevant and applicable in the long term.

Empowering Communities through Capacity Building

Enhancing the individual, organization and community capability through capacity development is key to the development discourse. Developing community capacity enables people to identify and develop the skills and resources they need to take control and improve their lives and empower their communities during the implementation of the project. If done correctly, this will impact and encourage sustainability of the project goals and achievements. Capacity building should therefore be seen as an important element in the planning, management and implementation of a project, and is an important variable that requires an investment in strategies at the onset to strengthen the exchange of information, knowledge and experience among different stakeholders. For capacity development to be achieved, all stakeholders must identify and appreciate its value in realizing true development. Supporting human development by quality education and emphasizing utilization and retention of existing capacities is important in catalysing capacity development by adopting a strategic approach to capacity building. This includes a sustained and systematic focus on conditions for retaining and employing local capacity in the design and implementation of projects such as PRP II, which is needed to ensure that individual, institutional and societal levels of capacity building are continually linked in the analysis, design and implementation of the project.

However, the emphasis placed on capacity development has been insufficient due to resource constraints. This means that greater creativity from the donor is needed to ensure that capacity development is built into the project as a medium of eradicating dependency by empowering the communities. This means that there needs to be more action with regard to the strategic capacity-building component for entities such as NSAs, which are important members in the development discourse. The inability to involve these individuals is as a result of budget restrictions, and so fewer of them can be accommodated within a call envelope. However, these actors have the best potential to sustain the gains of social development and the ability to encourage buy-in so as to encourage community development. This recommendation requires that more calls focusing on organizational capacity building as a theme are needed, so as to encourage community members to be involved in the process as active participants for change.

Knowledge is better gained when it is practised. Therefore, it is imperative that the European Union involves all stakeholders at all levels of the project cycle to develop the tools and skill sets to empower themselves and their communities. In addition, it is the utilization of local nationals in the implementation, monitoring and evaluation of the project that will encourage knowledge transfer and increase competency levels in this area. The use of non-nationals to conduct monitoring and evaluation activities was highlighted throughout the research as a recurring negative issue. The only medium to address this is to encourage both formal and informal training to assist in raising the knowledge of locals of the EU policies and procedures, to facilitate the rise of local experts. It cannot be reiterated enough that capacity development needs to employ a threefold approach:

1. Empowering the *individuals* with lifelong skills to function during and after the project. This can be achieved through formal and informal mediums of training;
2. Empowering the different *organizations* that aid in the implementation of the programme by investing in their capacity development at the initial stage of the project to enhance their competences and increase confidence; and
3. Empowerment of the *communities* by providing the necessary resources to raise the profile and competence level of the community to be active agents for change and authors of development.

All three are integral to the process and cannot be viewed in isolation. Therefore, this means that capacity-building activities and exercises must be built into the project with these three stakeholders in mind.

A diversification of persons that apply for funding is needed because it is often mainly faith-based organizations that participate in calls. Therefore, greater marketing needs to be done to attract more youth and community development organizations to want to be a part of PRPs. It is also important that the focus is more on soft projects as presented in the study. Soft projects such as parenting programmes, scholarships and internships will encourage capacity development and are proposed to be more impactful and sustainable.

Staff training activities are also directly linked to capacity building. However, these activities were underutilized in the capacity-building activities of NSAs. The information sessions, as a result, need to be used to direct attention to the opportunities for staff training in service delivery functions in PRP. Another approach that has been utilized by other international aid projects, such as the USAID COMET project, is sports. Sports is acknowledged as a powerful tool for youth inclusion and development policies. This approach can be used to assist in knowledge transfer utilizing an area of interest as a means to empower individuals.

JSIF should capitalize on its role as the lead implementing agency to document and promote the best practices of actions that are worth replicating. Therefore, the creation of a library or resource centre to serve as a repository of project information and implementation to address community empowerment, and provide models and best practices on how best to achieve community development is needed. Their involvement in these communities and the knowledge gained would be helpful in the implementation of other projects. This role is an important component in nurturing development actors in Jamaica, and can facilitate similar aid programmes that depend on similar models for project success. The strengthening of a results focus in capacity building to track progress and to clarify what is achievable over the short, medium and long term is needed to encourage sustainable projects, to empower communities and to raise their capacities. This can only be achieved if all stakeholders work effectively with other capacity-building institutions so as to share information on how and what works best, based on the cultural and local environment.

Empowering Communities through Community Leadership: A Prescribed Approach for Development

The ability to empower individuals has become a core principle for community development. The best approach seen by donor agencies to achieve development is through poverty alleviation, which strategy views the community as burdened socially and psychologically powerless, instead of providing aid relief to address some of the social issues and promote economic growth. Friedmann (1992) argued that development interventions should empower and mobilize poor households and communities for political participation on a wider scale. Only if people control their own destinies can long-term progress occur. For this to be done, the members of the communities need to be active in the empowerment process. One approach is through the mobilization of community organizations to assist in setting and achieving targeted empowerment goals. This study has noted that the communities in PRP II had sufficient CBOs that observed both the formal and informal structures of leadership. Therefore, the first step in empowering the community was to acknowledge these individuals and their roles and appreciate that they are a critical component in the empowerment and community development equation.

Often, these leaders lack capacity or material resources and have little training or education, but they are usually respected or feared by residents from the particular community over which they hold influence. They also have the ability to influence the views and perceptions of those who they lead. This suggests that there is no rigid code to becoming a community leader and anyone can be empowered to become a leader. The focus group discussion showed that these leaders emerged from some very unlikely situations. They often need help honing their skills, and encouragement to identify service opportunities.

Leaders come in all ages, sizes, shapes and genders. Therefore, another recommendation is to design and incorporate leadership training programmes and workshops that are diverse and that can incorporate various individuals, as part of the objectives for PRP programmes. This training would raise their knowledge of leadership and help to empower people to become more effective and efficient leaders. Based on the findings from the study, it was observed that these individuals had the power to decide whether a programme is accepted or rejected. They were often tasked with the responsibility to lead the charge by mobilizing community members to apply for the various grants, and by identifying community resources with assistance from the implementing agency and other agencies, such as the SDC.

Another critical area is motivating them to empower themselves since they often face several challenges that may affect their enthusiasm to lead these communities. Reference was made in previous chapters to the fact that their role as leaders is often questioned and scrutinized by their peers. This may result in a lack of support from those who are unable to identify and appreciate the need for community leaders. It is important that the European Union and JSIF identify these individuals as key stakeholders in the development discourse and indigenous measures be put in place to combat the abuse of their peers and encourage respect by reinstating the power lost in their ability to empower.

As observed, a number of CBOs that applied for these grants were from faith-based organizations. This speaks to the role of the church and the impact it has on the community. The church is often seen as another avenue to impact the lives of the community. Therefore, working in tandem with them is another medium by which these identified leaders can be empowered and motivated to lead, because there is usually a general respect for church and church leaders in these communities. This raises the question of whether empowered individuals become leaders or holding leadership positions empowers people (Zimmerman and Rappaport 1988). Leadership and empowerment are mutually reinforcing and both are interconnected; therefore, the approach taken must reflect this.

Training, support and empowering community leaders in these communities are needed, since social support and raising self-esteem and confidence will contribute to leadership competence. Confidence in one's leadership skills and a sense of mastery will raise self-esteem, which will be reflected in the approach taken to leadership. The ability to represent the needs of the communities in an articulate manner will be more accepted. It will also decrease the need for hand-holding because these people will be armed with community empowerment strategies to address problems that do not require substantial resources or expertise, since their own capacity would have been developed. Lack of capacity development is a major obstacle to successful community organization and this is primarily due to the lack of training in leadership development and organizational capacity development. This can only be achieved if there is greater participation and accountability by all stakeholders. This is needed to encourage and capture learning and shared empowerment of people.

Empowering Communities through Good Governance Structures

The positive impact that aid will have on development is dependent on sound economic management and the establishment of effective institutions. Established through strong governance structures, and by helping to fight corruption, improve transparency, and accountability of all stakeholders, these will strengthen and modernize established systems that will create an environment in which people are better able to empower themselves and their communities. The governance model should also be used as a medium of breaking down power. Addressing the underlying distribution of power will create spaces that facilitate open dialogue between all stakeholders, making them active participants in the development discourse. This addresses issues of transparency and accountability and how they are defined and translated into actions that will lead to impactful and sustainable projects that will empower these communities. The belief exists, as noted in the study, that a lack of good governance might be the main hindrance to sustained and impactful projects that are needed to encourage empowered communities and true development. This theory does in fact have some merit because good governance structures are needed to manage the process effectively and efficiently.

Additionally, for communities to be empowered, the good governance model must pay special attention to issues of equity and the inclusion of all stakeholders. As such, the needs and viewpoints of all – especially the beneficiaries of the programme – must be taken into account. Good governance should be judged by how well it is able to facilitate a process of inclusion and equity. This can only be achieved by addressing issues of power and control and allowing for the implementing agency to exercise some level of autonomy during the process; because currently, there are inequalities in the structure that exists among all stakeholders that are a part of the process. The vast majority of people that engage in these projects have a perception or model of what good governance should represent while addressing the issue of equity and inclusion. This includes the dismantling of highly concentrated structures of ownership; full employment; and access to basic infrastructure without the need to formalize themselves as registered organizations to access basic needs and infrastructural benefits, which are accorded to the privileged elites.

A good governance system is one that holds all parties involved accountable, a far cry from that which exists in the developing world. Hence, the prescribed approach to good governance cannot be an end in itself. It is an evolving process and has the potential to become a powerful instrument for radical transformation and change, if applied to all spheres of social life. Good governance cannot be entrenched or imposed by the donor agency. Instead it has to be imbibed, nurtured and cherished from within through the buy-in process. That is why the accountability approach needs to be a two-way process that facilitates all stakeholders being held to the same standards. For example, the European Union should also be held accountable to the community in the same way that the community and implementing agency are constantly reminded of the importance of being accountable to the European Union. If this is done, it will lead to positive results because the power dynamics would have been further broken down. It is important that one recognizes that power does exist both inside and outside the formal institutions.

Good governance must be characterized by its ability to encourage impactful projects that are sustainable and that can develop the capacities of individuals and communities with an end goal of empowering communities. Therefore, agencies such as the European Union must balance the social, economic and environmental needs of present and future generations through poverty and crime reduction. It is also important that power be shared to lead to equity and to increase access to decision making, priority setting and resource allocation processes. Access to information is fundamental to this understanding and to good governance. Human resources are the principal source of wealth for these communities; they are both the object and the means of sustainable human development; therefore, it is imperative that this capital be managed effectively, using the principles of good governance.

The State as an Actor for Community Empowerment

Good governance mandates that governments offer diligent, productive and transparent public services. However, the role of the state as a manager and provider of services and goods that meet the needs of the people has changed in an effort to achieve the continuous and complex demands of development. It is clearer that the success of a country's development programmes hinges on the country's effective economic policies, good governance and financial performance. Resolving the conflict between unlimited needs and wants on the one hand, and limited resources on the other, is the essence of development, and requires interventions from aid donors to provide citizens with an enabling environment that provides equal opportunities for a good life, which is the primary goal of the state (Toussaint and Comanne 1995). Improved government is needed that places the state as a facilitator, a mediator and as an active participant in the donor–recipient relationship (Toussaint and Comanne 1995). Governments must be encouraged to act in a way that demonstrates that they are being responsible, participative, transparent and accountable.

Another focal point is the responsibility of the state in the implementation and sustainability of high-impact projects. One challenge is the inability of government to be an active agent, or equal partner during the initial stages of a project that is targeted toward the needs of the intended beneficiaries. A positive that the state enjoys is its ability to assist with the coordination and management through the use of the PIOJ that acts in the capacity of the planning institution and provides oversight to the daily running of the project. However, the challenge also exists as the state is not always seen as an equal stakeholder due to the precarious position in which it is placed as being on the receiving end of aid, which limits the level of push back they may demonstrate due to this reliance. This is also a challenge because the government depends a lot on the aid provided by donor agencies to address the needs of its people. This lends itself to a cyclic approach as the government has an incentive to defer policy preferences such as the guidelines used, which can free them from the need to respond to their citizens. Aid also reduces the pressure on governments to be accountable to their citizens for how resources are utilized and leads to the erosion of accountability and responsiveness. Instead, strengthening the relationship between citizens and their governments is crucial for long-term, sustainable solutions that empower communities. Aid donors shouldn't replace the role of the state as a duty bearer responsible for providing the basic infrastructural needs, but instead the promotion of a partnership with the state, donors and the communities should be established to determine the prioritizing of funding that will have a lasting impact on the beneficiaries of the programme.

Empowering Communities through the Strengthening of Partnerships

For community empowerment to be achieved, emphasis needs to be placed on partnership and shared vision of all stakeholders. This vision, however, has to be jointly constructed and administered from a standpoint of collaboration and not imposition, consequently facilitating a shared ideology that is necessary to encourage project buy-in and appreciation for the universal concept of development. One approach to achieving this is through structural changes that can be arrived at through greater awareness and collaboration among partners. This will bring about greater political awareness and mobilization of the oppressed majority, not only by resisting and rejecting existing structures and ways of thinking, but also by building alternatives.

Community empowerment also speaks to the ability to strengthen communities by building local capacity and enhancing control. The use of partnership is also needed to diversify functional community groups and to expand the reach and scope of the project. From the study, it was noted that mostly faith-based organizations engaged the GOALA projects. The establishment of more community groups will result in long-term institutional arrangements with intersectoral, multicultural and multilevel community organizations such as youth groups, which can help to strengthen the community and will assist with prioritizing and creating areas of focal points that are more needs-driven. Modalities such as area-based employment and training projects will form part of the development agenda. These local partnerships will represent innovative strategies on the part of community groups and decentralize locally responsive governments and donors.

Partnership is also needed to combat the hierarchical structure held by donors who possess all the power. With the introduction of partnerships, a more inclusive and beneficiary-driven approach is accepted, since beneficiaries are seen as active agents in addressing and shaping socio-economic challenges and problems that were previously the sole responsibility of governments and donors. However, a key challenge of effective partnership was getting the right actors around the table because there existed several debates with regard to representation at the community level. Therefore, the selection process for representation needs to be transparent and inclusive. As was noted from the study that the partnership experience has evolved, and the need to involve diverse stakeholder viewpoints is critical to the discourse. The identification of relevant stakeholders and optimal inclusion is needed to achieve the purpose and goals of the project in realizing poverty alleviation and crime reduction.

In addition, the partnership must maintain a sense of balance between identifying common ground to hold the partnership together and encouraging variations to allow for complementarity of roles. In addition to describing shared purpose, partners should be encouraged to explore their disagreements, discuss to what extent it may be necessary to "agree to disagree" and explore in what ways the differences between them could contribute to achieving their common development goals. This approach is critical for the effective maximization of the limited resources while increasing accountability and ensuring that the projects have great impact and sustainability.

Revamping and Localizing the Text to Suit Our Cultural and Environmental Context

Many donor agencies have unsuccessfully tried to implement an off-the-shelf set of project management modules and guidelines that can fit all cultural and social environments without any challenges. However, this standard approach has proven to be unsuitable during project design, implementation and evaluation. While its purpose is to promote transparency, accountability and project success, the actual outcome has diverged from the original intent, since groups of voices were eliminated from the dialogue during the design. In addition to this, the focus was misdirected as more emphasis was placed on project outcomes and outputs as opposed to project impact. There was also a lowering of staff morale because people felt enslaved by the guidelines' processes and procedures. Therefore, a primary recommendation is for a more inclusive approach in the design and implementation of these projects to allow for more flexibility. The guide should be used as a support system for implementers, allowing them to exercise some amount of autonomy and flexibility during the project implementation phases.

The determination of project needs is another area of the guidelines that currently needs to be addressed because projects should be both demand and supply driven. Identification should not only be focused on the needs of the local entities but should also take into account the overall strategies of the government in particular, and donor agencies in general. Therefore, it would be important to consult a country's strategic documents (such as Jamaica's Vision 2030), to ensure that the efforts and goals of the donors are aligned with those of the country. The local needs for developing countries are great and it is critical that they not be ignored in an attempt to address global perceptions of poverty using standardized methodology. It is also difficult to meet all these local needs with the meagre resources available. Therefore, the prioritization process, based on established criteria, must be collaborative, engaging the intended beneficiaries, the developers of the guide, funders and implementing agencies. In addition, a prefeasibility test needs to be built into the guidelines as part of the initial activities to assist in the selection and assignment of the projects. Failure to do this can result in the inability to meet project objectives and goals.

In revamping the text, attention should also be paid to tailoring the localization of projects – identifying and referencing framework documents, standards and other relevant sources that provide processes, tools and techniques that are suitable for a particular venture. Tailoring is a process of customizing project management guidelines to suit the ever-changing needs of the intended population. A critical element in this is the modification of the existing procedures to meet the cultural and geographical needs of the intended beneficiaries. This approach will have a positive impact on the reach, scope and duration of the project along with its ability to adapt to the local environment.

The evaluation of donors by the beneficiaries, and their ability to collate all available inputs, including existing processes, assets and templates, user manuals and other supporting material will facilitate the smooth operation of the project. This is needed to eradicate critical modifications being made during the implementation of the project, which can have a severe impact on the development discourse with regard to project impact. Therefore, one possible approach is to first identify and understand the culture in which we operate, acknowledging that a one-size-fits-all method is not generally effective.

There are additional reasons that projects fail; therefore, a standard international model cannot be seen as the solution to the problem. Instead, the creation and fostering of better relationships among stakeholders and an understanding of their cultural practices and nuances need to be built-in to encourage project success. Also, flexibility and independence need to be extended to the implementing agencies after training is done, to facilitate the development of their capacity and restoration of their morale, eliminating a robotic approach to the process.

Effective communication needs to be viewed as a two-way process, since this is a vital component to the efficient utilization of the guide. The voices of all must be heard and reflected in the design of the guidelines, adhering to a policy of open communication, and encouraging all members to voice opinions and concerns.

As seen in previous chapters, communication is not transmitted through one medium but through several media; hence, it is important that written communication also be addressed. The guide needs to be written in a format that facilitates confidence by all stakeholders in its utilization. Throughout the study, several concerns were raised as to the way the guidelines were written and the jargon used in the writing of the text – making it cumbersome and difficult to interpret. In addition, the application forms to be completed by the beneficiaries of the project were quite tedious and posed several challenges for successful completion. In some cases, they were seen as a deterrent to application. They need to be simplified to better engage persons applying for these grants.

Monitoring and Evaluation: A Tool for Empowering Individuals and Communities

Accountability by donors can be more effectively represented by measuring changes in policies, resource allocations, changes in attitudes, values and practices, and the impact of these positive outcomes can be translated into improving the lives of poor and exploited persons during the implementation of these projects. It is therefore necessary to evaluate project outcomes and monitor project activities along with their objectives in order to ensure that project impact is achieved and positive changes occur in people's lives. The localized rights-based monitoring and evaluation approach was noted as a recommendation put forward to assist existing methods of measuring change. I am also mindful of recommending another international approach to address local problems. However, the approach that is recommended is one that takes into consideration cultural and environmental nuances to assist in the prioritization of actions. Providing evidence is the greatest opportunity for impact and sustainability to be achieved in the realization of human needs. This approach should be kept as simple and practical as possible.

However, throughout the research process, several persons interviewed spoke of the inability to properly monitor and evaluate project activities, outcomes and impacts. A recommendation put forward that could be adopted is a reward system for beneficiaries and implementers of the programme. This could also act as an incentive for the JSIF PRP II team to change its perception of how projects should be evaluated using the dimensions of change, to critically review and improve the impact and sustainability of these projects, therefore promoting a culture of accountability, participation and equity in practice.

Monitoring and evaluation should be conducted for the primary purposes – to measure impact, outputs, efficiency, effectiveness or change; to strengthen accountability; to facilitate learning; and to strengthen partnership among stakeholders. The ultimate aim of development is to bring about improvement in people's lives through individual and community empowerment. Measuring changes in people's lives is a key aspect of monitoring and evaluation. This information is needed to influence future decisions, and to encourage transparency and accountability of donors and implementers of the project. In order for people to be empowered, they have to understand what empowerment entails and how this can translate into improving their lives and how they fit into this ideal world portrayed for development. Access to information and transparency are critical to ensuring that services are delivered and standards are met in the quest for achieving this prescribed model.

Summary

From the study, it was observed that the EU guidelines and its use present several challenges during the project cycle. However, many questions arose: Do the identified positives outweigh the negatives? What lessons can we learn, implement or utilize from the positives? What lessons can we utilize in terms of how we overcome these identified hurdles and challenges?

In addition to this, several issues were raised with regard to the manual, process and procedure for project implementation and the impact that this has had on the development narrative. Issues were raised of aid dependency and the culture of dependency this has caused. A discussion around power formed a central part of the dialogue and the use of language and other discursive elements were examined. The need for a fundamental change was also seen as a key element for empowerment to be achieved. The author explored ways in which communities and individuals could become empowered, because true development can only be achieved when the individual and their community are empowered.

A fundamental change will only happen if many people demand it. The only way to demand this change is for all participants to first be seen as stakeholders with active voices, therefore strengthening their position as partners, which will result in them being treated as such. Donors must therefore engage both local implementers and beneficiaries of the projects in discussions, taking into consideration recommendations made, and provide some room for flexibility and creativity when utilizing the guidelines. This approach is needed, based on several cultural discourses that exist that have hampered project success.

Knowledge developed is knowledge learned. It is therefore important that capacity building and development are seen as important components in the development script. The expansion of individual, community and organizational capacity is needed for development to be achieved. It is the responsibility of donors to ensure that they provide the necessary tools and support to build capacity, including organization of previous project evaluation results that may act as a data source for best practices and help to identify future challenges and solutions that work. Aid agencies are also pressured to deliver and always have to justify their existence to their constituencies and to their donors. The pressure placed on these donors also results in collateral damage that forces them to insist on strict timelines of start and end dates with little to no room for flexibility. A more sustained relationship at the end of the project needs to be considered to generate better and lasting development results.

Donors also need to facilitate the implementation and commitment of aid ownership. If this is done, the project's efforts will become more sustainable and will have greater impact and reach. To improve ownership and project impact the beneficiaries of the project and the local implementing agencies must be brought in at the onset of the project to identify these needs and to ensure that these identified needs are at the centre of the development discourse. An impact assessment must be built into the project and there must be a shift in perception and focus that is needs-driven and centred around project impact with less emphasis being placed on project outcomes and outputs.

For impact to be the focal point of the development agenda, there also needs to be an incorporation of the local visions of the countries. For example, it is imperative that Jamaica's Vision 2030 forms part of the international development discourse that is observed locally as the development ideal. There is no aid without conditions; hence, donors need to provide development assistance that relates to beneficiary countries' national interest with the primary goal of having good achievement in social-economic development and poverty eradication.

The use of good governance practices, such as accountability, transparency and inclusiveness, is needed to encourage project and development success. As already discussed, one of the major challenges that affects countries like Jamaica is corruption, and the only way to minimize this is to ensure that these practices are adhered to. Commendation must be given to the European Union's approach to minimizing the incidence of corruption and misappropriation of funds based on its rigidity and enforcement of strict guidelines and penalties. Since there is no authentic aid ownership in development assistance, it is essential for partner countries to use all aid provided efficiently and effectively in order to encourage sustainable development programmes, and to get rid of the assumption that aid is a source of corruption. The utilization of continuous and indigenous monitoring and evaluation techniques is essential to the development discourse and special efforts should be made to ensure that this is built into the project from the conceptualization stage.

References

Ahmad, Ani Binti, Abu Daud bin Silong, Mina Abbasiyannejad and Turiman bin Suandi. 2014. "Roles and Issues of Village Development and Security Committee (VDSC) Institution for Rural Development in Malaysia". *Turkish Online Journal of Technology* 13 (3): F.

Andreasson, Stefan. 2010. *Africa's Development Impasse: Rethinking the Political Economy of Transformation*. London: Zed Books.

Arrowsmith, Sue Louise, and Martin Trybus. 2003. *Public Procurement the Continuing Revolution*. The Hague: Kluwer Law International.

Avdi, Evrinomy, and Eugenie Georgaca. 2009. "Narrative and Discursive Approaches to the Analysis of Subjectivity in Psychotherapy". *Social and Personality Psychology Compass* 3 (5): 654–70.

Bakker, Peter, and Klaus Leisinger. 2013. "The Key Challenges to 2030/2050: Mapping out Long-Term Pathways to Sustainability and Highlighting Solutions that should be Scaled Up". Background Paper for the High-Level Panel of Eminent Persons on the Post-2015 Development Agenda. Prepared by the co-chairs of the Sustainable Development Solutions Network Thematic Group on Redefining the Role of Business for Sustainable Development. http://unsdsn.org/wp-content/uploads/2014/02/The-Role-of-Business-Paper-for-HLP.pdf.

Barrett, Michele. 1997. "Ideology, Politics, Hegemony: From Gramsci to Laclau and Mouffe". In *Mapping Ideology*, edited by Slavoj Žižek, 243. London: Verso.

Bartle, Phil. 2003. "What Is Community? A Sociological Perspective". http://edadm821.files.wordpress.com/2010/11/what-is-community.pdf.

Becker, A.L. 1991. "Language and Languaging". *Language and Communication* 11:33–5.

Bell, William J. 2012. *Searching Behaviour: The Behavioural Ecology of Finding Resources*. The Netherlands: Springer Science and Business Media.

Bhargava, Vinay K., ed. 2006. *Global Issues for Global Citizens: An Introduction to Key Development Challenges*. Washington, DC: World Bank.

Biggs, S. 1999. "Community Capacity Building in Queensland: The Queensland Government Service Delivery Project". Unpublished paper. Office of Rural Communities, Brisbane, Queensland.

Binswanger, Hans P., and Swaminathan S. Aiyar. 2003. "Scaling Up Community-Driven Development: Theoretical Underpinnings and Program Design Implications". World Bank Policy Research Working Paper 3039. Washington, DC: World Bank.

Blair, Harry. 2000. "Participation and Accountability at the Periphery: Democratic Local Governance in Six Countries". *World Development* 28 (1): 21–39.

Boateng, Kofi Agyenim. 2009. "ICT-Driven Interactions: On the Dynamics of Mediated Control". PhD diss., London School of Economics and Political Science.

Bräutigam, Deborah A., and Stephen Knack. 2004. "Foreign Aid, Institutions, and Governance in Sub-Saharan Africa". *Economic Development and Cultural Change* 52 (2): 255–85.

Brett, Eduard A. 2003. "Participation and Accountability in Development Management". *Journal of Development Studies* 40 (2): 1–29.

Brigg, Morgan. 2002. "Post-development, Foucault and the Colonisation Metaphor". *Third World Quarterly* 23 (3): 421–36.

Brzezinski, Zbigniew. 2004. *Choice (Tercih)*. Istanbul: İnkıkap Kitapevi.

Burke, S., N. Murphy, C. Lanigan and L. Anderson. 2009. *An Asset-Based Community Development Approach to Skills-Banking and Capacity-Building in Toberona Dundalk*. Dublin: Combat Poverty Agency.

Callender, Guy, and Darin Matthews. 2000. "Government Purchasing: An Evolving Profession?" *Journal of Public Budgeting Accounting and Financial Management* 12 (2): 272–90.

Casley, Dennis, and Krishna Kumar, 1987. *Project Monitoring and Evaluation in Agriculture*. Baltimore: John Hopkins University Press.

Castro, Carlos J. 2004. "Sustainable Development Mainstream and Critical Perspectives". *Organization & Environment* 17 (2): 195–225.

Cooke, Bill, and Uma Kothari. 2001. *Participation: The New Tyranny*? London: Zed Books.

Cowen, Michael P., and R. W. Shenton. 1996. *Doctrines of Development*. London: Routledge.

Cunningham, Gord, and Alison Mathie. 2002. "Asset-Based Community Development: An Overview". Workshop proceedings at the Asset-Based Community Development Workshop, Bangkok, Thailand.

DAC (Development Assistance Committee). 1996. *Shaping in the 21st Century: The Contribution of Development Co-operation*. Paris: OECD.

Dale, Reidar. 2004. *Development Planning: Concepts and Tools for Planners*. London: Zed Books.

Davies, Bronwyn, and Rom Harré.1990. "Positioning: The Discursive Production of Selves". *Journal for the Theory of Social Behaviour* 20 (1): 43–63.

Denis, Goulet. 1977. *The Cruel Choice: A New Concept in the Theory of Development*. New York: Athenium.

DFID (Department for International Development). 2002. *Tools for Development. A Handbook for those Engaged in Development Activity*. London: Performance and Effectiveness Department, DFID.

Durning, Alan B. 1989. *Action at the Grassroots: Fighting Poverty and Environmental Decline*. Washington, DC: Worldwatch Institute.

Eade, Deborah. 2010. *Deconstructing Development Discourse: Buzzwords and Fuzzwords*, edited by Andrea Cornwall and Deborah Fade. Warwickshire, UK: Practical Action/Oxfam GB.

Eade, Deborah, and Jo Rowlands. 2003. *Development Methods and Approaches: Critical Reflections – Selected Essays from Development in Practice*. Oxford: Oxfam GB.

Easterly, William. 2003. "Can Foreign Aid Buy Growth?" *Journal of Economic Perspective* 17:23–48.

EC (European Commission). 2004a. "Agreement No. 9646/JN Financing Agreement between the European Commission and Jamaica Poverty Reduction Program 2 (JM/002/04) EDF101/Sector 2-Financing Procedures and ROM/Financing Agreement/fed/jm/002-04(9)".

———. 2004b. "Aid Delivery Methods: Project Cycle Management Guidelines". *Supporting Effective Implementation of External Assistance*. https://ec.europa.eu/europeaid/sites/devco/files/methodology-aid-delivery-methods-project-cycle-management-200403_en_2.pdf.

———. 2010. "EU Development Policy in Support of Inclusive Growth and Sustainable Development: Increasing the Impact of EU Development Policy". Green Paper COM(2010) 629 final. http://eur-lex.europa.eu/legal-content/EN/TXT/?uri=celex:52010DC0629.

———. 2013. "Directorate General for Development and Cooperation: European Aid, Practical Guide to Procedures for Programme Estimates (Project Approach) Version".

———. 2014. "Practical Guide for Procurement and Grants for European Union Track Change Version". https://ec.europa.eu/europeaid/2014-practical-guide-procurement-and-grants-european-union-external-actions-track-change-version_en.

Emmerij, Louis. 2010. "The Basic Needs Development Strategy". Background paper. World Economic and Social Survey. http://www.un.org/en/development/desa/policy/wess/wess_bg_papers/bp_wess2010_emmerij.pdf.

Escobar, Arturo. 1992. "Planning". In *The Development Dictionary: A Guide to Knowledge as Power*, edited by Wolfgang Sachs, 132–45. London: Zed Books.

———. 1995. "Anthropology and the Future: New Technologies and the Reinvention of Culture". *Futures* 27 (4): 409–21.

———. 1996. "Power and Visibility: The Invention and Management of Development in the Third World". University Microfilms International, Ann Arbor, Michigan.

———. 1997. "The Making and Unmaking of the Third World through Development". In *The Post-development Reader*, edited by Majid Rahnema and Victoria Bawtree, 85–93. London: Zed Books.

———. 2000 "Beyond the Search of a Paradigm? Post Development and Beyond". *Development* 43 (4): 11–14.

——. 2006. "Difference and Conflict in the Struggle over Natural Resources: A Political Ecology Framework". *Development* 49 (3): 6–13.

Esteva, Gustavo, and Madhu Suri Prakash. 1998. *Grassroots Post-modernism: Remaking the Soil of Cultures*. London: Zed Books.

European Union Action Aid. 2008. "Human Rights-Based Approaches and European Union Development Aid Policies". http://www.terredeshommes.org/wp-content /uploads/2013/01/HRBA-Briefing-Paper-Sept-FINAL.pdf.

Evans, Peter, Dietrich Reuschmeyer and Theda Skocpol. 1985. *Bringing the State Back In*. Cambridge: Cambridge University Press.

Eyben, Rosalind. 2006. *Relationships for Aid*. London: Earthscan.

Fairclough, Norman. 1993. "Critical Discourse Analysis and the Marketization of Public Discourse: The Universities". *Discourse and Society* 4 (2): 133–68.

——. 1995. *Media Discourse*. London: E. Arnold.

——. 2000. *New Labour, New Language?* London: Routledge.

——. 2001. *Language and Power*. Harlow, UK: Pearson Education.

——. 2003. *Analysing Discourse: Textual Analysis for Social Research*. Routledge: Taylor and Francis.

Fairclough, Norman, Phil Graham, Jay Lemke and Ruth Wodak. 2004. "Introduction", *Critical Discourse Studies* 1 (1): 1–7. http://www.csun.edu/~vcspcoog/604/intro -critdiscourse.pdf.

Fairclough, Norman, and Ruth Wodak. 1997. "Critical Discourse Analysis". In *Discourse Studies: A Multidisciplinary Introduction*, edited by T. van Dijk, 258–84. London: Sage.

Fawcett, Stephen B., Glen W. White, F. E. Balcazar, Yolanda Suarez-Balcazar, R. Mark Mathews, Adrienne Paine-Andrews, Tom Seekins and John F. Smith. 1994. "A Contextual-Behavioral Model of Empowerment: Case Studies Involving People with Physical Disabilities". *American Journal of Community Psychology* 22 (4): 471–96.

Federal Acquisition Institute. 1999. *The Federal Acquisition Process*. Washington, DC: Federal Acquisition Institute.

Ferguson, James. 1990. *The Anti-Politics Machine: Development, Depoliticization, and Bureaucratic Power in Lesotho*. Minneapolis: University of Minnesota Press.

Forrester, Simon, and Irem Sunar. 2011. *Developing and Managing EU Funded Projects, Technical Assistance for Civil Society Organisations*. Potoklinica, Bosnia and Herze-govina: TACSO Regional Office.

Foucault, Michel. 1980. "Truth and Power". In *Power/Knowledge Selected Interviews and Other Writings,* edited by Colin Gordon; translated by Colin Gordon, Leo Marshall, John Mepham and Kate Soper. New York: Pantheon.

——. 1998. *Madness and Civilization: A History of Madness in the Age of Reason*. London: Penguin.

Fowler, Alan. 2002. "Organizing Non-profits for Development". In *The Earthscan Reader on NGO Management*, edited by M. Edwards and A. Fowler, 74–85. London: Earthscan.

Friedmann, John. 1992. *Empowerment: The Politics of Alternative Development*. Cambridge, MA: Blackwell.

Gardner, John W. 1990. "Leadership and the Future". *Futurist* 24 (3): 8.

Garriado, Marley, Sey Araba and Hart Tabita S. 2012. "Exploratory Study on Explanations and Theories of How Telecenters and Other Community Based E-inclusion Actors Operate and Have an Impact on Digital and Social Inclusion Policy Goals". European Commission, Joint Research Center, Institute for Prospective Technological Studies. San Jose State University. http://scholarworks.sjsu.edu/cgi/viewcontent.cgi?article.

Gavas, E., N. Memon and D. Britton. 2012. "Winning Cybersecurity One Challenge at a Time". *IEEE Security and Privacy* 10 (4): 75.

Gaventa, Beverly Roberts. 2003. *The Acts of the Apostles*. Nashville: Abingdon Press.

Girvan, Norman. 2007. *Power Imbalances and Development Knowledge*. Ottawa: North-South Institute.

Goeppinger, Amy. 2002. "The Fallacies of Our Reality: A Deconstructive Look at Community and Leadership". *International Journal of Leadership in Education* 5 (1): 77–83.

Green, Duncan. 2012. *From Poverty to Power: How Active Citizens and Effective States can Change the World*. 2nd ed. Oxford: Oxfam. http://policy-practice.oxfam.org .uk/publications/from-poverty-to-power-2nd-edition-how-active-citizens-and -effective-states-can-249411.

Gregory, Derek. 1998. *Geographical Imaginations*. Cambridge: Blackwell.

Guijt, Irene, and MeeraKaul Shah, eds. 1998. *The Myth of Community: Gender Issues in Participatory Development*. London: Intermediate Technology.

Haferkamp, Hans, and Neil J. Smelser. 1992. *Social Change and Modernity*. Berkeley: University of California Press.

Harvey, David. 1996. *Justice, Nature and the Geography of Difference*. London: Blackwell.

Heck, Bernard Van. 2003. *Participatory Development: Guidelines on Beneficiary Participation in Agricultural and Rural Development*. Rome: FAO.

Heller, Peter S., and Sanjeev Gupta. 2004. "More Aid: Making It Work for the Poor". In *Helping Countries Develop: The Role of Fiscal Policy*, edited by Sanjeev Gupta, Gabriela Inchauste and Benedict Clements, chap. 15. Washington, DC: IMF.

Herbert, Ross. 2006. *Africa after Aid: Engineering an End to Dependency*. Johannesburg: Brenthurst Foundation.

Heywood, Andrew. 2007. *Political Ideologies: An Introduction*, 4th ed. New York: Palgrave Macmillan.

Hickey, Samuels, and Giles Mohan, eds. 2004. *Participation: From Tyranny to Transformation? Exploring New Approaches to Participation in Development.* London: Zed Books.

Hofstede, Geer, and Robert McCrae. 2004. "Culture and Personality Revisited: Linking Traits and Dimensions of Culture". *Cross-Cultural Research* 38:52–88.

House, Robert, Mansour Javidan, Paul Hanges and Peter Dorfman. 2004. "Understanding Cultures and Implicit Leadership Theories across the Globe: An Introduction to Project GLOBE". *Journal of World Business* 37 (1): 3–10.

Hummelbrunner, Richard, and Harry Jones. 2013. "A Guide to Managing in the Face of Complexity". Working Papers, Overseas Development Institute, London.

Hydén, Göran, Julius Court and Kenneth Mease. 2004. *Making Sense of Governance: Empirical Evidence from Sixteen Developing Countries.* Boulder: Lynne Rienner.

IFAD (International Fund for Agriculture Development). 2009. "Occasional Papers Knowledge for Development Effectiveness, Sustainability of Rural Development Projects Best Practices and Lessons Learned by IFAD in Asia". https://www.ifad.org/documents/10180/538441f4-bb55-4e99-9e23-854efd744e4c.

Israel, Barbara A., Barry Checkoway, Amy Schulz and Marc Zimmerman. 1994. "Health Education and Community Empowerment: Conceptualizing and Measuring Perceptions of Individual, Organizational, and Community Control". *Health Education and Behavior* 21 (2): 149–70.

James, Kariuki. 2014. "An Exploration of the Guiding Principles, Importance and Challenges of Monitoring and Evaluation of Community Development Project and Programmes". *International Journal of Business and Social Science* 5 (1): 140–47.

JSIF (Jamaica Social Investment Fund). 2006. "Operations Manual". Revised. http://www.jsif.org/sites/default/files/JSIF%20Operations%20Manual_1.pdf.

Kanstrup-Jensen, Annette. 2006. "Development Theory and the Ethnicity Question: The Cases of the Lao People's Democratic Republic and Thailand". PhD diss., Faculty of Social Sciences, Aalborg University.

Kaufmann, Daniel, Aart Kraay and Massimo Mastruzzi. 2008. "Governance Matters VII: Aggregate and Individual Governance Indicators 1996–2007". Policy Research Working Paper no. 41–49. Washington, DC: World Bank. http://papers.ssrn.com/sol/3/paperscfn?abstract-id=965077.

Kiely, Ray. 1999. "The Last Refuge of the Noble Savage? A Critical Assessment of Post-development Theory". *European Journal of Development Research* 11:30–55. doi:10.1080/09578819908426726.

Koser, Khalid. 2010. "Introduction: International Migration and Global Governance". *Global Governance* 16 (3): 301–15.

Kreisberg, Seth. 1992. *Transforming Power: Domination, Empowerment, and Education.* Albany: State University of New York Press.

Kretzmann, John P., and John McKnight. 1993. *Building Communities from the Inside Out: A Path toward Finding and Mobilizing a Community's Assets.* Evanston, IL: Center for Urban Affairs and Policy Research, Neighborhood Innovations Network, Northwestern University.

Lancaster, Carol. 2007. *Foreign Aid: Diplomacy, Development, Domestics Politics.* Chicago: University of Chicago Press.

Latouche, Serge. 1989. *Under-Development Is a Form of Deculturation.* Auckland, NZ: Department of Economics, University of Auckland.

Levinson, David, and Karen Christensen. 2003. *Encyclopedia of Community: From the Village to the Virtual World.* Vol. 3. Thousand Oaks, CA: Sage.

Luke, Allan. 2002. "Beyond Science and Ideology Critique: Developments in Critical discourse Analysis". *Annual Review of Applied Linguistics* 22:96–110.

Lukes, Steven. 1994. *Power: A Radical View.* London: Macmillan.

Mastruzzi, Massimo. 2009. "Governance Matters VIII: Aggregate and Individual Governance Indicators for 1996–2008". World Bank Policy Research Working Paper No. 4978. Washington, DC: World Bank.

Matland, Richard E. 1995. "Synthesizing the Implementation Literature: The Ambiguity-Conflict Model of Policy Implementation". *Journal of Public Administration Research and Theory* 5 (2): 145–74.

McKinlay, Robert D., and Richard Little. 1979. "The US Aid Relationship: A Test of the Recipient Need and Donor Interest Models". *Political Studies* 27 (2): 236–50.

Miles, Matthew B., and A. Michael Huberman, eds. 1994. *Qualitative Data Analysis: An Expanded Sourcebook.* Thousand Oaks, CA: Sage.

MNSJ (Ministry of National Security and Justice). 2013. *Citizen Security and Justice Programme Baseline Study.* Kingston: MNSJ.

———. 2017. "Strategic Crime Brief to the Joint Select Committee". MNSJ, Kingston, Jamaica.

Moncrieffe, Joy. 2010. "Poverty Reduction Programme II Technical Assistance-Non-state Actors Assessment Study". EU/ PIOJ: Study for Non-state Actors Programme in Jamaica: A.R.S Prgetti S.P.A in Country Evaluation Jamaica. Final Report, vol. 1: Main Report, September.

Mosse, Roberto. 1996. "Performance Monitoring Indicators Handbook". World Bank Technical Paper no. 334. World Bank, Washington, DC.

Moyo, Dambisa. 2009. *Dead Aid: Why Aid Is Not Working and How There Is Another Way for Africa.* London: Penguin.

Munck, Ronaldo, and Denis O'Hearn. 1999. *Critical Development Theory: Contributions to a New Paradigm.* London: Zed Books.

NCYD (National Centre for Youth Development). 2013. "Auditor General's Department Activity Based Audit Report". NCYD, Kingston, Jamaica.

Nascimento, Ana Paul. 2017. *Funding Matters: A Study of Internationlization Programs in Science, Technology, and Innovation*. Sweden: Media-Tryck, Lund University.

Nicholas, John M., and Herman Steyn. 2008. *Project Management for Business, Engineering, and Technology: Principles and Practice*. Amsterdam: Elsevier.

Nustad, Knut G. 2001. "Development: The Devil We Know?" *Third World Quarterly* 22 (4): 479–89. doi:10.1080/01436590120071731.

Nye, Joseph S. 2002. *The Paradox of American Power: Why the World's Only Superpower Can't Go It Alone*. Oxford: Oxford University Press.

Oakley, Peter. 1991. *Projects with People: The Practice of Participation in Rural Development*. Washington, DC: International Labour Organization.

OECD (Organization of Economic Cooperation and Development). 2000a. *DAC Journal 2000: France, New Zealand, Italy* 1 (3). Paris: OECD. http://dx.doi.org /10.1787/journal_dev-v1-3-en.

———. 2000b. "Informal Checklist of DAC and Related Activities, Keyed to the Development Co-operation Programme of Work", as of 30 September 2000. http://www .oecd.org/officialdocuments/publicdisplaydocumentpdf/?cote=DCD/DAC(2000)1 /REV2&docLanguage=En.

Page, Nanette, and Cheryl E. Czuba. 1999. "Empowerment: What Is It?" *Journal of Extension* 37 (5): 1–5.

Parfitt, Trevor W. 2002. *The End of Development? Modernity, Post-modernity and Development*. London: Pluto Press. http://public.eblib.com/choice/publicfullrecord .aspx?p=3386179.

Patras, Panagiotis, and Vaios Koutis. 2010. *Participatory Mapping: Methodology and Guidelines Using the Bottom-Up Approach Method*. Crossing Generations Crossing Mountains. Kenakap SA, Greece: European Union Lifelong learning.

Perkins, Douglas D., and Marc A. Zimmerman. 1995. "Empowerment Theory, Research, and Application". *American Journal of Community Psychology* 23 (5): 569–79.

Pieterse, Jan Nederveen. 2000. "After Post-development". *Third World Quarterly* 21 (2): 175–91. doi:10.1080/01436590050004300.

———. 2001. "Participatory Democratization Reconceived". *Futures* 33 (5): 407–22. doi:10.1016/S0016-3287(00)00083-5.

Pigg, Kenneth E. 1999. "Community Leadership and Community Theory: A Practical Synthesis". *Community Development* 30 (2): 196–212.

PIOJ (Planning Institute of Jamaica). 2007. *Economic and Social Survey Jamaica (2009–2012)*. Kingston: PIOJ.

———. 2016 *Economic and Social Survey Jamaica (2013–2015)*. Kingston: PIOJ.

PIOJ/STATIN 2012 (Planning Institute of Jamaica and Statistical Institute of Jamaica). *Jamaica Survey of Living Conditions*. Kingston: PIOJ.

Potter, Johnathan. 2003. "Discourse Analysis and Discursive Psychology". In *Qualitative Research in Psychology: Expanding Perspectives in Methodology and Design*, edited by Paul Camic, Jean E. Rhodes and Lucy Yardley, 73–94. Washington, DC: American Psychological Association.

Pretty, Jules N., Irene Guijt, John Thompson and Ian Scoones. 1995. *Participatory Learning and Action: A Trainer's Guide*. London: International Institute for Environment and Development.

Putnam, Robert D. 2007. *Bowling Alone: The Collapse and Revival of American Community*. New York: Simon and Schuster.

Rabinow, Paul A. 1991. *The Foucault Reader: An Introduction to Foucault's Thought*. London: Penguin.

Rahnema, Majid. 1991. *Global Poverty: A Pauperizing Myth*. Montreal: Intercultural Institute of Montreal.

———. 1997. "Towards Post-development: Searching for Signposts, a New Language and New Paradigms". In *Development: Identities, Representation, Alternative*, edited by Stuart Corbridge, 377–403. London: Taylor and Francis.

Ramalingam, Ben, Harry Jones, Toussaint Reba and John Young. 2008. *Exploring the Science of Complexity: Ideas and Implications for Development and Humanitarian Efforts*, vol. 285. London: Overseas Development Institute.

Randel, Judith, and Tony German. 1998. *The Reality of Aid: An Independent Review of Poverty Reduction and Development Assistance*. London: Earthscan.

Randel, Judith, Tony German and Deborah Ewing. 2002. *The Ageing and Development Report: Poverty, Independence, and the World's Older People*. London: Earthscan.

Rappaport, Julian. 1985. "The Power of Empowerment Language". *Social Policy* 16 (2): 15–21.

Redclift, Michael R. 2005. "Sustainable Development (1987–2005): An Oxymoron Comes of Age". *Sustainable Development* 13:212–27.

Remenyi, Judit. 2004. "What Is Development?" In *Key Issues in Development*, edited by K. Damien, J. Remenyi, J. Mckay and J. Hunt, 2. New York: Palgrave Macmillan.

Reno, William. 1998. *Warlord Politics and African States*. Boulder: Lynne Rienner.

Riddell, Roger C. 2007. *Does Foreign Aid Really Work?* Oxford: Oxford University Press.

Roche, Chris JR. 1999. *Impact Assessment for Development Agencies: Learning to Value Change*. Oxford: Oxfam.

Rocheleau, Dianne, and Rachel Slocum. 1995. "Participation in Context: Key Questions". *Power, Process and Participation: Tools for Change*. London: Intermediate Technology.

Rodrigues, Ivete, and Roberto Sbragia. 2012. "The Cultural Challenges of Managing Global Project Teams: A Study of Brazilian Multinationals". *Journal of Technology Management and Innovation* 8:4–4. doi:10.4067/S0718-27242013000300004.

Rostow, Walt Whitman. 1960. *The Stages of Economic Growth: A Non-Communist Manifesto*. Cambridge: Cambridge University Press.

Sabran, Mohammad Shatar. 2003. *An Introduction to Community Development and Leadership*. Malaysia: Universiti Putra Malaysia Press.

Sachs, Jeffrey. 2002. "Resolving the Debt Crisis of Low-Income Countries". *Brookings Papers on Economic Activity* 1:257–86.

Sachs, Jeffrey, John W. McArthur, Guido Schmidt-Traub, Margaret Kruk, Chandrika Bahadur, Michael Faye and Gordon McCord. 2004. "Ending Africa's Poverty Trap". *Brookings Papers on Economic Activity* (1): 117–240.

Sanyal, Bishwapriya. 1988. "The Myth of Development from Below". Department of Urban Studies and Planning, MIT, Cambridge, MA. http://web.mit.edu/sanyal/www/articles/Myth%20of%20Dev.pdf.

Schuurman, Frans J. 2000. "Paradigms Lost, Paradigms Regained? Development Studies in the Twenty-First Century". *Third World Quarterly* 21 (1): 7–20.

Seers, Dudley. 1969. *The Meaning of Development*. Brighton, UK: Institute of Development Studies at the University of Sussex.

Sen, Amartya. 1999. *Development as Freedom*. New York: Knopf.

Shah, Anup. 2012. "Foreign Aid for Development Assistance". *Global Issues* 25. http://www.globalissues.org/article/35/foreign-aid-development-assistance.

Shepherd, Andrew. 1998. *Sustainable Rural Development*. London: Macmillan.

Shihata, Ibrahim. 1981. "The OPEC Fund for International Development". *Third World Quarterly* 3 (2): 251–68.

Simon, Marilyn K., and Jim Goes. 2011. *Developing a Theoretical Framework*. Seattle: Dissertation Success.

Singh, Kunwar D., and S.M. Nyandemo. 2004. *Aspects of Project Planning, Monitoring, Evaluation and Implementation*. Dehradun, India: Bishen Sighn.

Spicker, Paul. 2008. *Social Policy: Themes and Approaches*. London. Policy Press.

Srebrnik, Henry. 2000. "Can an Ethnically-Based Civil Society Succeed? The Case of Mauritius". *Journal of Contemporary African Studies* 18 (1): 7–20.

Staudt, Kathleen. 1991. *Managing Development: State, Society, and International Contexts*. Newbury Park, CA: Sage.

Stoecker, Randy. 2012. *Research Methods for Community Change: A Project-Based Approach*. Los Angeles: Sage.

Stokke, Olav. 2009. *UN and Development: From Aid to Cooperation*. Bloomington: Indiana University Press.

Storey, Andy. 2000. "Post-development Theory: Romanticism and Pontius Pilate Politics". *Development* 43 (4): 40–46.

Sutton, Paul. 2005. *Caribbean Development and Overview*. Swiss Caribbean Chamber of Commerce. http://swisscaribbean.org/?i=10.

Thai, Khi V. 2001. "Public Procurement Re-Examined". *Journal of Public Procurement* 1 (1): 9–50.

Theodoulou, Stella Z., and Chris Kofinis. 2004. *The Art of the Game: Understanding American Public Policy Making*. Belmont, CA: Wadsworth.

Tienhoven, Nicovan. 2009. "Mid-Term Evaluation of the Poverty Reduction Programme II (PRPII) Jamaica. Letter of Contract N2009/216546". Jamaica Social Investment Fund Archives, Kingston.

Titscher, Stephan, Michael Meyer, Ruth Wodak and Eva Vetter. 2000. *Methods of Text and Discourse Analysis*. London: Sage.

Toussaint, E., and D. Comanne. 1995. "Globalization and Debt". *Notebooks for Study and Research* 24/25. http://www.iire.org/node/211.

United Nations. 2011. *Social Development in an Uncertain World UNRISD Research Agenda (2010–2014)*. Geneva: UNRISD. http://www.unrisd.org/research-agenda.

———. 2015. "Transforming Our World: The 2030 Agenda for Sustainable Development". https://sustainabledevelopment.un.org/post2015/transformingourworld.

UNDP (United Nations Development Programme). 2005. *Human Development Report 2005: International Cooperation at a Crossroads: Aid, Trade and Security in an Unequal World*. New York: UNDP.

———. 2010. *The Real Wealth of Nations. Pathways to Human Development*. 20th anniversary ed. New York: Palgrave Macmillan.

UNDP, United Nations Population Fund and United Nations Office for Project Services. 2011. "Country Programmes and Related Matters: 2012–2016". http://www.undp.org/content/dam/jamaica/docs/researchpublications/poverty/CPDJamaica2012-2016.pdf.

Van Dijk, Jan. 2001. "Modelling of Plasma Light Sources: An Object-Oriented Approach". PhD diss., Technische Universiteit, Eindhoven.

Vincent, John W, II. 2009. "Community Development Practice". In *An Introduction to Community Development,* edited by Rhonda Philips and Robert Pittman, 167–96. London: Routledge.

Volgy, Thomas J., Derrick V. Frazier and Robert S. Ingersoll. 2003. "Preference Similarities and Group Hegemony: G7 Voting Cohesion in the UN General Assembly". *Journal of International Relations and Development* 6:51–70.

WCED (World Commission on Environment and Development). 2002. *Our Common Future*. Oxford: Oxford University Press.

Wetherell, Margaret, Stephanie Taylor and Simeon Yates. 2001. *Discourse Theory and Practice: A Reader*. London: Sage.

Widdowson, Henry George. 2007. *Discourse Analysis*. Vol. 20. Oxford: Oxford University Press.

Wilkinson, Richard G. 2005. *The Impact of Inequality: How to Make Sick Societies Healthier*. New York: New Press.

Williams, Daniel, and Norman McIntyre. 2001. "Where Heart and Home Reside: Changing Constructions of Place and Identity". *Trends 2000: Shaping the Future: The 5th Outdoor Recreation and Tourism Trends Symposium*, compiled by Kim Luft and Sandy MacDonald, Sandy, 392–403. East Lansing, MI: Department of Parks, Recreation and Tourism Resources, Michigan State University.

Wodak, Ruth. 2001. "The Discourse-Historical Approach". In *Methods of Critical Discourse Analysis*, edited by Ruth Wodak and Michael Meyer, 63–94. Los Angeles: Sage.

World Bank. 2006. "Understanding Socio-economic and Political Factors to Impact Policy Change". World Bank, Social Development Department, International Bank for Reconstruction and Development Report No. 36442-GIB, November, Washington, DC.

———. 2011. "Beyond Economic Growth: Globalization and International Trade". http://www.worldbank.org/depweb/beyond/beyondco/beg_12.pdf.

World Vision. 2002. *Transformational Development Indicators Field Guide*. Washington, DC: World Vision Development Resources Team.

Yule, George. 2006. *The Study of Language*. Cambridge: Cambridge University Press.

Ziai, Aram. 2004. "The Ambivalence of Post-Development: Between Reactionary Populism and Radical Democracy". *Third World Quarterly* 25 (6): 1045–60. doi: 10.1080/0143659042000256887.

———. 2007. *Exploring Post-development: Theory and Practice, Problems and Perspectives*. London: Routledge.

Zimmerman, Marc, and Julian Rappaport. 1988. "Citizen Participation, Perceived Control, and Psychological Empowerment". *American Journal of Community Psychology* 16:725–50.

Index

CPSIA information can be obtained
at www.ICGtesting.com
Printed in the USA
LVHW010002290722
724651LV00003B/368

9 789766 408480